THE SNAKE

Three Millennia of Anti-Semitism

Yitzhak Q. Rosenthal

The Snake: Three Millennia of Anti-Semitism
by Yitzhak Q. Rosenthal

ISBN 978-1-64550-503-7

CONTENTS

This book is part of a 2019 decalogue consisting of

- Sign of Times: Music Anthology and Lyric Analysis
- Hollywood Misogyny
- Beginners' Guide to the FED:
  Why it is Unique on our Planet
- The Kennedy Kurse: Four Obvious Konnektions
- Manichaeism and Satanic Child Abuse
- Progressive Intolerance: Last Stop Before Hitler
- Patriotic Ingenuousness
- Deism versus Theism:
  2-7 in the Scientific Arena of the 20th Century
- Feminine Feminist:
  A Missing Link Eluding Discovery
- The Snake: Three Millennia of Anti-Semitism

"I love the Jews"
J.M Escrivá de Balaguer y Albás

INTRODUCTION

What is the Snake?

The snake is the symbol of evil, in general, and of the devil, for Christians. Its theological significance is explained in the separate book of "Appendices to the Snake", in Appendix 3, though it can be skipped without loss of readability of this book. Appendices 1 and 2 are a necessary prerequisite before even starting to read the first chapter of this book. Appendix 1 contains the Table of Contents of the so-called "Protocols of the Meetings of the Learned Elders of Zion". I here summarize the main three characteristics of their ideology:

(i) First, its principal goal is world dominion for a few elected Jewish people, and the absolute submission of the rest of humanity (the "Goyim" or "Gentiles" or "non-Jews", plus all non-elected Jews). The protocols explain how to achieve this goal: by moral destruction of the Gentile culture, to such extent, that Gentiles will be reduced to numb slaves under the superior Jewish race. Although the mafia's goal is fixed since the very beginning (long term absolute world dominion), the protocol methods change continually, because they reflect the conclusion of regular meetings of the "Learned Elders of Zion". These Protocols are a mere mafia's "reference book", explaining to the mafia élite (and to nobody else) how the main goal is to be achieved. Of course, today one does not speak about Synagogues anymore, except in the sense of a Jewish Temple and its faithful.[1] Let me state this clearly from the beginning: *the protocols are not a "Jewish manuscript", but a "manuscript of a specific Jewish mafia".* That is, it implies no dishonor whatsoever for the large majority of the Jewish people. I love the Jewish people, and I hate EZ, whether Jewish or not.[2] Much to the contrary: *the*

---

[1]   Half the Acts of the Apostles tell the history of Paul and Barnabas being continually persecuted by those mafias. The cities they were expelled from were not Jewish, of course. They were all gentile. With one peculiarity: everywhere, the Synagogue formed a highly respected power center. Not only those located in the present-day Turkey, but also those in present-day Greece (Athens and Thessaloniki). While honest Jews experienced the dispersion as a punishment of God for their ancestors' infidelity, the mafias abused of the Jewish dispersion to penetrate gentile power structures all over the world. Obviously, they kept strict supervision over which Jews were allowed to move.

[2]   This is much the same in every country in this world: they all have their own mafias, which, in matters moral, have nothing whatsoever in common with the people of their birth country. Let me mention but a simple example of moral perversion.

ordinary, honest, virtuous Jews are usually the most
abused of by the mafia as mere disposable tools to
reach their goals. For this reason, I make a clear
distinction between the honorable Jewish people on

The Israeli army decides towards the end of the 20th century
to use Sarin gas in large quantities. Since the use of Sarin is
easily traceable, they start a smear campaign against their two
neighbor victims, i.e., Syria and Iraq. In the UN meeting about
Iraq, American general Colin Powell, secretary of state (2001-
2005) under G.W. Bush, declares aloud that American
military photos leave no doubt as to Iraq's preparing chemical
weapons (read Sarin) for a war against Israel. Powell was
booed by some UN members, and openly laughed at by Dick
Cheney, before just before Powell began his speech. Of course,
half ingenuous Christianity protests against Iraq. Finally,
Saddam Hussein swallows his mega-pride and admits a
European Investigation Commission on his grounds. Alas, too
late. Hussein had already been eaten by EZ. The fact is that
not a single European seems to remember, today, that the
UN-coordinated International Investigation Committee found
nothing in Iraq: all the sites shown on Powell's photos were
mere dumps or empty halls. Meanwhile, Israel was importing
huge amounts of Sarin ingredients (via Amsterdam Schiphol,
the main airport of my country) for many years. They had
accumulated so much stuff that they could intoxicate the
African continent three times to death. Mistakes happen: an
El-Al plane crushes into a Dutch residential area with high
risers. No problem for EZ. In less than ten minutes the impact
zone swarms of Mossad agents. Only ten years later do we
unofficially know that they were looking for chemical
ingredients of Sarin. In my EZ-brainwashed country, this is
considered an anti-Semitic argument. After a year of pre-
brainwashing by EZ-channels Washington Post and New York
Times, Israel finally attacks Iraq, and accuses Saddam
Hussein for using Sarin gas against Israel. Some 90% of
ingenuous Christians swallow that misinformation like a
sweet pie. When ten years later exactly the same occurs
between Israel and Syria, Christians appear to have learnt
nothing from the Iraq "civil war". This will not change in
about ten years from now, when Israel (or rather its American
puppet army) will destroy Iran, in the name of peace and
humanity.

one hand, and an abject Jewish mafia on the other hand. In Jesus' time, the Saducee High-Priests of the Synagogues were not only fake religious leaders of the faithful, but also foremost members of local mafias. In the Acts of Apostles there are plenty of proofs for this interpretation. A first one is Chapter 6, verse 9: "Then certain people came forward to debate with Stephen, some from Cyrene and Alexandria who were members of the synagogue called the Synagogue of Freedmen, and others from Cilicia and Asia." If synagogues were mere Jewish Temples, they would carry the names of their respective cities. The name Synagogue of Freedmen indicates something more is going on. The Synagogue of Jerusalem seems to have ordered their freedmen colleagues to start an argument with Stephen, such that after their argument, the Sadducees of Jerusalem could stone Stephen to death. Yet another example. The argument used by the Synagogue of Thessalonica (Acts of the Apostles 17, 5-8), that the Christians broke Caesar's edict by claiming that a long time ago crucified man was their King, whose primary endeavor was to throw Tiberius Caesar off his throne, was exactly the same as that used against Jesus by the Synagogue of Jerusalem. Ergo, the Synagogues were not primarily Houses of Prayer, as already made explicit by Jesus' expelling all traders from the Temple Court, but they were primarily local mafias, with a clearly defined hierarchy and well-maintained contacts between them.

(ii) Second, EZ is much smarter and much more patient than every other mafia. Whether we speak of Russians or Italians, they are all amateur improvisers as compared to EZ. The previous Mossad's shield summarized very aptly EZ's secret weapon: "For by deceit and perversion thou shalt wage war" (a free translation of Proverbs 24:6). Some years ago they decided to replace it by a less revealing quote of Proverbs. Yet that is their strategy: make Goyim believe what EZ fakes, and pervert morality to the point that Goyim cannot defend themselves anymore. Ford's comments on the protocols are reproduced integrally in Appendix 2.[3] According to Protocol map illustrating the snake's itinerary through history (not shown in this book, but described in words by Henry Ford, see page 62 of this book), the snake's six major victories occurred in the following cities and years:

---

3   As I already wrote, the only difference in our wording of world history, is that where Ford speaks of the International Jew, I speak of the international EZ-Mafioso. Although the highest levels in EZ are occupied by traceable Jewish bloodlines, non-Jewish members committed to EZ's goals can reach the highest charges and responsibilities: just think of George Soros. The big difference between the selected bloodlines and the "freemasonic cattle" (EZ-executives like George Soros) is that the former will never make themselves known, while the "freemasonic cattle" is at full display (see Protocol 11, number 7).

- **Athens, 429 BC:** EZ convinced Pericles to prepare for a Peloponnesian War; it resulted in an irrational and irreparable enmity between ancient Athens and Sparta
- **Rome, 69 BC:** EZ conspired in overthrowing the Republic in favor of an Empire
- **Madrid, 1552:** EZ prepared a Peace Treaty of Augsburg, which would tear up Europe in heavily frustrated Christian denominations
- **Paris, 1789:** EZ convinced Robespierre and colleagues to start a Revolution that would create an irrationally deep hatred between Catholics and non-Catholics
- **London, 1814:** EZ prepared the Congress of Vienna, such that it would tear the Habsburg Empire into multiple pieces, waging war on each other
- **Berlin, 1871:** EZ's Franco-Prussian peace would lead to World War I;
- **St. Petersburg, 1881:** EZ's assassination of Alexander II would prepare the ground for a Bolshevik uprising.

(iii) *Third, the protocols were never supposed to go public.* They were meant as a secret document, exclusively for the very select club members.

I admit it is not easy to keep those documents secret for three millennia. A single disgusted Elder of Zion is enough to make them go public. However, I do not ask the reader to believe the here presented interpretation of the Protocols on my own authority, but on that of Henry Ford sr., the last "Goy"4 who could still compete on an equal business level with the Extreme Zio*nist mafia.*

---

4   Hebrew for "heathen"

CHAPTER 1

Hitler's Willing Victims

All Germans were not Hitler's willing *executioners*, as some EZ-terrorist claims, but exactly the opposite: *A few* Germans were Hitler's willing *victims.*

1.1 Lutheranism

The disgrace of Lutheranism was its birth certificate, "cuius regio, eius religio", officially agreed upon in 1555 in Augsburg. This principle was originally meant merely to give legitimacy to Lutheranism. But at what cost! It was the very opposite of the teachings of the Christ, who said to "give to Caesar what is his, and give to God what is His". Christ said in a few words that, as far as taxes are concerned, both have to be satisfied in the name of two different rules: the earthly and the Divine. And as far as the freedom to choose one's own convictions, Christ always showed the highest respect for other people's choices, although he would not refrain from commenting, as in case of the young rich man, that his refusal to give up all earthly goods would not only make him sad in this world, but would make him unable to choose God in afterlife.

The anti-Christian venom of the Augsburg Treaty would later extend to all protestant religions. Clearly, Calvin's style of ruling left no doubt that he considered the Augsburg Treaty as a political means to force all Swiss in his Canton to convert to Calvinism. He issued the order to burn a former friend of his on the stake, because of his "heretic opinions". The surprise of his friend, who burnt at the stake with Calvin overseeing the execution, was a clear sign that Calvin had given a radical turn in his life: A turn from intellectual debate to imposing convictions onto other people.

The practical interpretation of the Augsburg Treaty was hereby mutated, by its own proponents, from a decree of official Catholic recognition of the natural and supernatural legitimacy of other Christian Creeds, to the blunt imposition of whatever Creed on whatever people. From then on, every (theocratic) Monarch was free to impose his own protestant religion onto all his subjects.

History shows that in all protestant states, this interpretation ended up in a strongly theocratic world vision, *thereby setting the clock back by at least two millennia*: as if the Christ had not lived at all, as if He had not saved us from bondage and slavery.

Calvin went as far as embracing the full-fledged Muslim-like theocracy, wherein the Monarch-Bishop represented both the civil and religious highest powers concentrated in a single man: This is both intolerant and severely discriminating towards women, who, in Calvin's eyes, would never play a significant political role.

Quite oppositely, in Catholic states the Augsburg Treaty ended up to be interpreted as the loss of all Divine election claims by the Monarch, thereby opening the way to the modern Christian interpretation of the division of powers: earthly power in the "Trias Politica"[5], and Divine power in the Hierarchy of a Church one freely chooses to adhere to. In later times, such tolerance of a citizen's free choice would be extended to dissociation from all possible Christian Creeds. This is quite simple to understand for anybody who managed to free him or herself from the 18th century obscurantist prejudices and historical claims.[6]

Why would I speak out so vehemently against obscurantism? The reason is simple. Obscurantism is the secretive collection of a group of terrorists that want to take over full power by manipulation and deceit: both the religious power of public catechesis and ointment of earthly rulers, as the earthly power, by introducing the "Deep State" concept. This way, the obscurantist terrorists could rule the world without people even having seen their real rulers.

On the other hand, obscurantism unwittingly achieved a huge benefit for the Catholic Church: it taught the Church to abandon all its political ambitions, and to

---

5   This trias was first clearly formulated by the 18th century
     French philosopher, Charles Montesquieu
6   called "Enlightenment" by those very obscurantists

deeply review its own doctrine of the separation of Church and State, to that point, that the once huge Vatican would eventually reduce to a militarily not defendable, extremely small piece of land, at the mercy of its host, Italy.

Summarizing, the Treaty of Augsburg helped Catholics in understanding Christ's reply to the tax collector, whence in their essential separation of two domains of power: the earthly domain, which is mainly about the power to require taxes in exchange for the organization of public services, like national highways, other means of transport, and defense.

For our protestant brothers, it had the quite negative consequence of identifying the secular leader with God's rule over the country. The worst example of this belief was the German vote on Hitler in 1932: All Protestants voted for Hitler, and all Catholics against, as proved in the two maps below.

Several Popes heroically resisted the slow but merciless shrinking of the Vatican State, once covering half the Italian peninsula, down to a mere suburb of Rome. With the advantage of posterior judgement, one could say they were mistaken.[7] God never wanted armies for his Church, but prayer and fulfillment of the New Law.

---

7   Of course, this theological mistake does not reduce their sanctity in any way, as what they did was always conform the Law if the New Testament, and for love of the Mystic Body of Christ (an alternative term designing the Catholic Church).

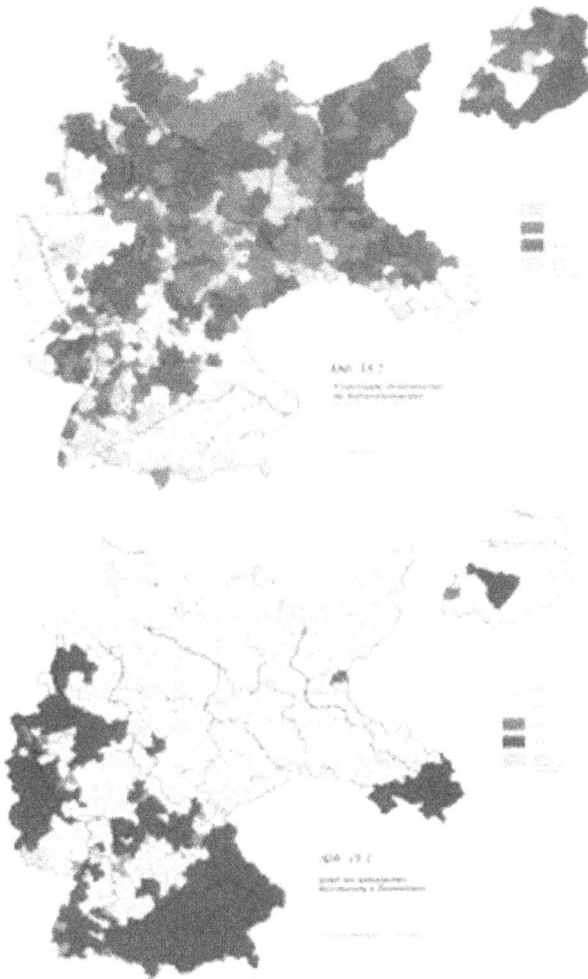

Figure 1: Geographical distribution of pro-Hitler voting percentages (upper panel) and of the Catholic population density (lower panel) in 1932. The anti-correlation applies even to the smallest enclaves.

I apologize for the low quality of the maps, but such maps are obviously very hard to find on the web.[8]

Ecumenism tries to bring people together, not to drive them apart. Hence, it should start by putting the historical facts on the table, assessing them, and ask forgiveness where needed: Catholics to the Protestants, because influential Catholics considered them outlaws before 1555, and German Protestants to German Catholics, for having brought shame over Germany. As long as these facts remain undiscussed and apologies are not pronounced, ecumenism reaches little farther than an endless exercise in Jesuit mind restriction.[9] Only upon truth can progress in unity thrive.

1.2 The EZ-Hitler Deal

Hitler's *Mein Kampf* is the compilation of two different political manifestoes. He wrote the first volume in 1924 in the Bavarian fortress of Landsberg am Lech, where he was imprisoned after his early-aborted Beer-Hall Putsch of 1923. It treats the world of Hitler's youth, the First World War, and the "betrayal" of Germany's collapse in 1918; it also expresses Hitler's racist ideology, identifying the

---

8 EZ deletes most of these posts. The remaining ones are deleted by intolerant Lutherans and retarded Catholics.

9 An example of "Jesuit mind restriction" is answering "no, I never had any part in it" while *thinking by yourself* the following sentence continuation: "as far as you are entitled to know". It is nothing but a blunt lie, hypocritically hidden by a conscience sweetener.

Aryan as the "pure" race and the Jew as the "parasite." Please understand me well, reader, that I have equal problems like you with believing that a Jewish mafia is able to plan all this hatred towards Jews.[10]

Hitler wrote the second volume after his release from prison in December 1924. It outlines the political program, including the terrorist methods, which National Socialism must pursue both in gaining power and in exercising it thereafter in the new Germany.

In 2010 Jean-Paul Mulders, a Belgian journalist, and Marc Vermeeren, a historian, tracked down Hitler's relatives, including an Austrian farmer who was his cousin, earlier this year. The Y-chromosome E-M35, which showed up in their samples, is rare in Western Europe and is most commonly found in the Berbers of Morocco, Algeria and Tunisia, as well as among Ashkenazi and Sephardic Jews. Saliva samples, taken from 39 relatives of Hitler, point to Jewish ancestors. Hitler's father, Alois Hitler, possibly is the illegitimate offspring of a maid called Maria Schickelgruber and a Jew called Frankenberger.

Actually, many people make jokes about Hitler possibly being 25% Jewish. I do not mind: they have the right. On the other hand, I have the right to take the issue at face value, and to ask the serious question: how could

---

10   I firmly believe (that is, I have not the tiniest piece of evidence to prove) that all so-called "Catholic anti-Semitism" over the centuries was not only a true historical fact, but that it was being fueled continuously by the Sadducee mafia, who wanted nothing but solid proof that Christians were anti-Semites.

so many German Lutherans believe Hitler's story about Aryanism, when *his mere looks* were all but Aryan? The only possible answer is that those Germans were profoundly frustrated. They would take any leader, even the satan himself, in order to re-establish their humiliated self-respect.

This takes us to an important set of questions:

- Who paid Hitler's *Wirtschaftswunder*?
- Who paid his brainwashing propaganda?
- Who paid his military expenses?
- What made Hitler so sure that he could march into the French-occupied Rheinland without a single protest?
- Why did prime ministers Arthur Neville Chamberlain, Édouard Daladier, Benito Mussolini and his foreign minister Galeazzo Ciano, give Hitler the Czechoslovakian Sudetenland for free?

Two historical facts should be clear by now:

- The Exchequer of the German Confederacy went technically bankrupt in 1918.
- At the time of the München betrayal of Czechoslovakia, EZ owned all war loans extended to all WW I countries. Hence, their leaders had their hands tied.

Chamberlain, Daladier, Hitler, Mussolini, and Ciano, the infamous cosignatories of the 1938 München betrayal of Czechoslovakia

Do we have a multinational conspiracy theory here, according to which the three most powerful European leaders simultaneously suffered a mental stroke, which made them simultaneously decide to give a little ugly impotent worm all the means to turn Europe into one big monument for fallen soldiers and civilians? So my dear reader, whatever your own conspiracy theory, at least check if it is able to explain the allied behavior in München. Particularly the French, who were still painfully restoring from their World War I wounds?

*Neville Chamberlain amidst his enthusiastic followers,
waving his self-written, Hitler-applauded fraternity
declaration. Hitler considered Chamberlain's
declaration as well-suited for use in his private toilet.*

Of course, you will try to convince me that Daladier and
Chamberlain *loved* to please the little ugly worm. I guess
the name of the radical-leftist Édouard Daladier, who
correctly predicted that Hitler's ambitions annihilated
those of Napoleon, will gradually disappear from the
history books of *La France*. Wikipedia's writer of the 1938
München betrayal is so ingenuous as to believe that
Daladier's repulsion to whatever concession to Hitler was
due to pressure exerted on him by Chamberlain. Even
though all historians would agree on such an idiotic

interpretation, I cannot help laughing aloud. What could Chamberlain possibly give to France? His cowardice? His near bankruptcy? His pathetical impotence? All three München conspirators had immense EZ-loans, and were much too busy licking their WW I wounds. The wiki-genius continues his account:

> Daladier had already been made aware in 1932, through German rivals to Hitler, that Krupp was manufacturing heavy artillery and the Deuxième (French for second) Bureau had a grasp of the scale of German military preparations, but lacked hard intelligence of their hostile intentions.

So we have to believe poor Daladier "lacked hard intelligence of Hitler's hostile intentions"? What would such evidence look like, anyway? A kind of written declaration of intent? Or an appendix to Mein Kampf, mentioning "Please, my leftist brother in arms, remind that I mean what I wrote"?

These historians are either idiots (which I do not believe) or simple mercenaries of EZ. I call upon you to either stop profaning Wikipedia sites, or to use at least a single brain cell of yours before writing down such extreme nonsense. Daladier was *obviously* fully aware of the German threat, and *had no illusion at all* with respect to Hitler's intentions, given that he had already compared them to Napoleon's. Ok, he was a leftist. But that is not equal to being dumb, nor is it a reason for automatic Divine pardon.

As mentioned before, winners write history. in this case, EZ and its mercenaries. They will keep their mouth tightly shut about the negotiations preceding the 1938 München betrayal. To my big surprise, I managed to catch the wiki-genius on a passage that actually makes sense:

> In October 1938, Daladier opened secret talks with the Americans on how to bypass American neutrality laws and allow the French to buy American aircraft to make up for productivity deficiencies in the French aircraft industry. Daladier commented in October 1938, "If I had three or four thousand aircraft, Munich would never have happened," and he was most anxious to buy American war planes as the only way to strengthen the French Air Force. A major problem in the Franco-American talks was how the French were to pay for the American planes, as well as how to bypass the American neutrality acts. In addition, France had defaulted on its World War I debts in 1932 and hence fell afoul of the American Johnson Act of 1934, which forbade loans to nations that had defaulted on their World War I debts. In February 1939, the

French offered to cede their possessions in the Caribbean and the Pacific together with a lump sum payment of 10 billion francs, in exchange for the unlimited right to buy, on credit, American aircraft. After tortuous negotiations, an arrangement was worked out in the spring of 1939 to allow the French to place huge orders with the American aircraft industry; though, as most of the aircraft ordered had not arrived in France by 1940, the Americans arranged for French orders to be diverted to the British.

Clearly, the ingenuous French failed to realize that Hitler's biggest financer lived in the US, and that all military deals passed through the Rothschild family. EZ nodded "yes" but meant "over my dead body". That is the only real reason for the "American betrayal" of Europe's anti-Hitler forces, and not Daladier's paperwork on Hitler's intentions. Note that the betrayal, being "American", had nothing whatsoever to do with the American people, but was perpetrated exclusively by EZ, who owned the US since at least 1913.

Summarizing, we presently have a choice between a mega-conspiracy, involving four different regimes on one hand, and on the other, a minuscule conspiracy of some hundred blood-related men *with a common goal*. Look at how others get immediately smeared by the label "anti-Semite" upon writing something like I propose here. My simple conspiracy theory has no need of thousands of "coincidences". The politically correct mega-conspiracy, of three countries, rabidly opposed to Hitler's taking universal power, which caused the war by trying to avoid it, was made up by EZ for the weak minds. In reality, EZ owned Hitler's loaner banks.[11] In 1920 it was already in full control of England, France, and Italy. Rothschild's Extreme-Zionist mafia was not only repulsively rich and globally influential; *it also had at least 24 centuries of experience in toppling or destabilizing legitimate regimes, in causing depressions in order to have their power instruments like the FED installed, and subsequently in bringing down a country by imposing ridiculous interest rates on her debts to EZ.* Hence, the Hitler-EZ deal was simple: Hitler uses the Marx- and Darwin-derived theories of race superiority (all EZ-financed and EZ-promoted doctrines), gets to rule Germany as a Savior during a decade, convinces the German army to eliminate itself, and orders to kill as many European Jews as possible. In return, EZ finances all of Hitler's operations, receives the outrageous interests, and confiscates all European-Jewish savings, as no European Jew is to survive World War II. Why would

---

11   A more detailed, but definitely inconclusive, report on Hitler's financiers is available at web site https://www.bibliotecapleyades.net/sociopolitica/wall_street /chapter_07.htm, involving people like Hugo Stinnes, Fritz Thyssen, Albert Voegler, Adolph and Emil Kirdorf, Kurt von Schröder, the Schneider Group, Roland Harriman, H.J. Kouwenhoven, J.G. Gröningen, C Lievense, E.S. James, A. Steinke, Karl Lange, and F. Springorum

EZ proceed in such a complicated, hardly self-consistent way, as it would later allow the Americans to free Europe from the Führer, and its own protocols swear to help out the Jewish people? Well, hardly self-consistent this is only to ingenuous patriots. From EZ's point of view, they killed five birds in one shot, which is pretty consistent.

1. Whatever the costs of a European war, all implied countries would have to pay back their EZ-loans after the war, with a dazzling interest rate. What was EZ's financial risk? Zero, because they loaned equal amounts to both sides.

2. The Rothschild mafia would moreover appropriate all European-Jewish savings, as all account-holders would have ceased to exist after WW II.

3. All post-war Jewish Holocaust institutes were nothing but Rothschild's puppets. Still today, many Christian Germans suffer a guilt complex, because they do not understand that *they are not the primary cause, but the primary victims of World War II.*

4. The war increased EZ's fortune by a factor between 5 and 100.[12] After the war, EZ has been increasingly rubbing in the Germans' guilt complex, and patently milking the German economy, because of an alleged *German-only* guilt in provoking World War II. Some EZ-pundits even dare to write down such nonsense,

---

12   this fraction is difficult to estimate due to the complete absence of serious historical investigation

for which they should be tried and convicted.[13] *It was not Germany, nor the Germans, but the Hitler-EZ deal, which caused WW II.*

5. EZ would strengthen its grip on the Jewish community.

Simplistic readers might ask whether the writer of this book is anti-Semitic. Obviously not: Jews are not the only Semites. Palestinians are no less Semites. Well then, is the writer anti-Jewish? Again, not, as this book only attacks an extremely small Jewish minority: The Sadducee mafia. It does not think of blaming *Jews indiscriminately*. I love all Russians except Russian mafias milking Spanish beaches. *Likewise, I love all Jews*, except the putrid animal Mr. Rothschild, who sold his soul to the devil.[14] I love the Jews even more for the following reason: *while the Russian mafias do not own the Russian people, EZ does own all Jews*. The righteous Jews (a very large

---

13   See, for example, EZ-puppet's Daniel Goldhagen's book "Hitler's Willing Executioners", 1996. EZ should have paid a little more for such a job, and pick a thorough historian instead of a quasi-pundit. Well, this is the direct consequence of avarice. The same happened a month before 9/11, when EZ wanted huge revenues on worthless, squalid, old-fashioned twin towers, by means of a security contract, which included terroristic attacks.

14   Like EZ-clown Jared Kushner. He rose to national prominence after trying to purchase building 666 of the fifth Avenue. He threw in 1.8 billion dollars, which was an unheard of quantity at the time.

majority, by mere statistics) therefore have the inhuman choice between either death-for-the-sake-of-divine-election, or executing EZ's wishes (with understandably deep regret and moral aversion).

1.3 Eastern Germany under Russian Domination

So, what do you think is the author's intentions in writing down this apparently anti- ecumenist chapter? Well, my first intention is to relieve 90% of the Germans from their supposed guilt. The second one is to warn Americans that exactly the same is happening to them, now, as what happened to Germany before World War II. The third intention is helping the readers to understand that the snake makes no difference at all between communism and dictatorship. "les extrèmes se touchent" (extremes touch one another), is a popular French saying. I would rather formulate it as "les extrèmes s'embrassent" (extremes embrace one another). This is what movie director/writer Lars Kraume understood better than anybody else, when in his 2018 movie[15] "Das schweigende Klassenzimmer" he

---

15   The title of Lars Kraume's movie ("Das schweigende
      Klassenzimmer", the silent classroom) is a wordplay that,
      exceptionally, translates to all languages. The silent one is
      obviously not the classroom, but the East-German teenagers
      in it. The 1956 Hungarian Revolution (five years before the

has one of the high-school students shout out: "but these are Gestapo methods!" For the younger readership: The Gestapo[16] was Hitler's National Secret Police, while the SSD[17] or popularly called "Stasi" was the Russian-Communist supervised East-German National Security Service. According to the high-school student, the Stasi used the same methods Gestapo. If there be any historical truth in this movie-claim, from where the similarity in methods? Because Hitler once thought it funny to invite

---

construction of the Berlin Wall) inspires most of them to stage a five-minute wordless protest, leaving their teacher puzzled as to why his pupils do not answer any of his questions. He interprets this as a mutiny. Since every action in East Germany was considered to be inherently political, the teenagers' odd behavior is initially investigated by the headmaster, later by the Education Board and finally by the Education Minister himself. The schoolboy who took the initiative (Theo) told his best friend (Kurt) that he left for West-Germany, in order to save all his classmates from immediate expulsion from the school. He entrusted Kurt with protecting their mates, such that all of them would eventually obtain their high-school degrees. After being interrogated by the East-German Secret Service of the Department of Education, Kurt simply says to his schoolmates: "Now it's everybody for one's own. Don't make yourself any illusions. For sure, whoever decides to leave for West Germany, do it in couples, so that one can tell any misfortunes of his/her companion to his family." The last shots of the movie are taken in the train to West Germany. When Kurt enters a train wagon with his mate, he looks around, stupefied, as he realizes that all his mates took the same decision: to leave for the West. Quite unwittingly, he did keep his word to Theo. Oh yes, about the wordplay: the teenagers leave behind an empty classroom, with nobody left to speak.

16   Geheime StaatsPolizei
17   StaatsSicherheitsDienst

the Russian Secret Service to inspect his Gestapo? Only the golden hedges of our world are able to think along such monstrously meandering lines.

In my view, there was no such thing as a *similarity* in the first place: there was strict *identity*. Hitler's Gestapo and Honecker's[18] Stasi were strictly identical, because they were both owned and organized by EZ: their methods are still in use, to date, by the Israeli secret services with respect to the Palestinians, in their cursed "prisons",[19] and on that abject EZ-site called Guantanamo Bay. Wikipedia explains:[20]

> Following World War II, Soviet leader Joseph Stalin headed a group of nations on his Western border, the Eastern Bloc, that then included Poland, Hungary and Czechoslovakia, which he wished to maintain alongside a weakened Soviet-controlled Germany. As early as 1945, Stalin revealed to German communist leaders that he expected to slowly undermine the British position within the British occupation zone, that the United States would withdraw within a year or

---

18   The East-German dictators before Erich Honecker were
      Walter Ulbricht and Wilhelm Pieck
19   read "torture clinics"
20   https://en.wikipedia.org/wiki/Berlin_Wall

two, and that nothing would then stand in the way of a united communist Germany within the bloc. The major task of the ruling communist party in the Soviet zone was to channel Soviet orders down to both the administrative apparatus and the other bloc parties, which in turn would be presented as internal measures. Property and industry were nationalized in the East German zone. If statements or decisions deviated from the described line, reprimands and (for persons outside public attention) punishment would ensue, such as imprisonment, torture and even death. Indoctrination of Marxism-Leninism became a compulsory part of school curricula, sending professors and students fleeing to the West. The East Germans created an elaborate political police apparatus that kept the population under close surveillance, including Soviet secret police (Smersh). The German Democratic Republic (East Germany) was declared on 7 October 1949. By a secret treaty, the Soviet Ministry of Foreign Affairs accorded the East German state administrative authority, but not autonomy. The Soviets permeated East German administrative, military and secret police structures and had full control.

Although the common use is to speak about "the Soviets", I would like to spare the Russian people, who have nothing whatsoever to do with the usurpation of East Germany. I would rather speak of the EZ-founded and EZ-controlled "Soviet Bolshevism", which is even more ultra-left than Hitler and Mussolini combined.

That Mussolini's Fascism and Hitler's Nazism are ultra-right, is a plain historical lie invented by Leftists. They are easily recognizable: their sect denies anything in detriment of leftism, *independently of historical facts*. Leftists suffer an international blindness, where patriots suffer a national blindness.

Rightists in general accept responsibility for historical misdoings on their ideology's account. The sectarian aspect of leftism is also easily recognizable: the leftist sect thinks that anger and insult are the only way to respond to rightist arguments, while rightists at least seem to have the illusion that an intellectual discussion with a leftist should be possible.

However, the sad truth is that a change of impressions is impossible with leftists, as it is with any other sectarian people or institutions. Sectarian institutes are all those where "you can check in every time you like, but you can never leave" (quote stolen from the Eagles' Hotel California). The most influential sects are: Muslim theocracies; some pseudo-Christian denominations like puritanism or scientology; the socially self-gettoing Jewry; and higher-degree freemasonic cults.

CHAPTER 2

Common Patterns in Civil Wars

2.1 The Russian October Revolution (1917)

The Wikipedia page on Lenin opens as follows:[21]

Vladimir Ilyich Ulyanov (22 April 1870[1] – 21 January 1924), better known by the alias Lenin, was a Russian communist revolutionary, politician, and political theorist. He served as head of government of Soviet Russia from 1917 to 1924 and of the Soviet Union from 1922 to 1924. Under his administration, Russia and then the wider Soviet Union became a one-party communist state governed by the Russian Communist Party.

---

21   https://en.wikipedia.org/wiki/Vladimir_Lenin

Ideologically a Marxist, he developed political theories known as Leninism. Born to a wealthy middle-class family in Simbirsk, Lenin embraced revolutionary socialist politics following his brother's 1887 execution. Expelled from Kazan Imperial University for participating in protests against the Russian Empire's Tsarist government, he devoted the following years to a law degree. He moved to Saint Petersburg in 1893 and became a senior Marxist activist. In 1897, he was arrested for sedition and exiled to Shushenskoye for three years, where he married Nadezhda Krupskaya. After his exile, he moved to Western Europe, where he became a prominent theorist in the Marxist Russian Social Democratic Labor Party (RSDLP). In 1903, he took a key role in a RSDLP ideological split, leading the Bolshevik faction against Julius Martov's Mensheviks. Encouraging insurrection during Russia's failed Revolution of 1905, he later campaigned for the First World War to be transformed into a Europe-wide proletarian revolution, which as a Marxist he believed would cause the overthrow of capitalism and its replacement with socialism. After the 1917 February Revolution ousted the Tsar and established a Provisional Government, he returned to Russia to play a leading role in the

October Revolution, in which the Bolsheviks overthrew the new regime.

Lenin's October Revolution continues as follows:[22]

In a diplomatic note of 1 May, the minister of foreign affairs, Pavel Milyukov, expressed the Provisional Government's desire to continue the war against the Central Powers "to a victorious conclusion", arousing broad indignation. On 1–4 May, about 100,000 workers and soldiers of Petrograd, and after them the workers and soldiers of other cities, led by the Bolsheviks, demonstrated under banners reading "Down with the war!" and "all power to the soviets!" The mass demonstrations resulted in a crisis for the Provisional Government. 1 July saw more demonstrations, as about 500,000 workers and soldiers in Petrograd demonstrated, again demanding "all power to the soviets", "down with the war", and "down with the ten capitalist ministers". The Provisional Government opened an offensive against the Central Powers on 1 July, which soon collapsed. The news of the offensive

_____

22   https://en.wikipedia.org/wiki/October_Revolution

and its collapse intensified the struggle of the workers and the soldiers. A new crisis in the Provisional Government began on 15 July. On 16 July, spontaneous demonstrations of workers and soldiers began in Petrograd, demanding that power be turned over to the soviets. The Central Committee of the Russian Social Democratic Labor Party provided leadership to the spontaneous movements. On 17 July, over 500,000 people participated in what was intended to be a peaceful demonstration in Petrograd, the so-called July Days. The Provisional Government, with the support of Socialist-Revolutionary Party-Menshevik leaders of the All-Russian Executive Committee of the Soviets, ordered an armed attack against the demonstrators, killing hundreds. A period of repression followed. On 5–6 July, attacks were made on the editorial offices and printing presses of Pravda and on the Palace of Kshesinskaya, where the Central Committee and the Petrograd Committee of the Bolsheviks were located. On 7 July, the government ordered the arrest and trial of Vladimir Lenin. He was forced to go underground, as he had been under the Tsarist regime. Bolsheviks were arrested, workers were disarmed, and revolutionary military units in Petrograd were disbanded or sent to the war front. On 12 July, the Provisional Government published a law introducing the death penalty at the front. The second coalition government was formed on 24 July, chaired by Alexander Kerensky. Another problem for the government centered on General Lavr Kornilov, who had been Commander-in-Chief since 18 July. In response to a Bolshevik appeal, Moscow's working class began a protest strike of 400,000 workers. They were supported by strikes and protest rallies by workers in Kiev, Kharkov, Nizhny Novgorod, Ekaterinburg, and other cities. In what became known as the Kornilov affair, Kornilov directed an army under Aleksandr Krymov to march toward Petrograd to restore order to Russia, with Kerensky's agreement. Details remain sketchy, but Kerensky appeared to become frightened by the possibility the army would stage a coup, and reversed the order. By contrast, historian Richard Pipes has argued that the episode was engineered by Kerensky. On 27 August, feeling betrayed by the government, Kornilov pushed on towards Petrograd. With few troops to spare on the front, Kerensky turned to the Petrograd

Soviet for help. Bolsheviks, Mensheviks and Socialist Revolutionaries confronted the army and convinced them to stand down. The Bolsheviks' influence over railroad and telegraph workers also proved vital in stopping the movement of troops. Right-wingers felt betrayed, and the left wing was resurgent. With Kornilov defeated, the Bolsheviks' popularity in the soviets grew significantly, both in the central and local areas. On 31 August, the Petrograd Soviet of Workers and Soldiers Deputies, and on 5 September, the Moscow Soviet Workers Deputies adopted the Bolshevik resolutions on the question of power. The Bolsheviks won a majority in the Soviets of Briansk, Samara, Saratov, Tsaritsyn, Minsk, Kiev, Tashkent, and other cities. [...]

On 20 December 1917 (2 January 1918 new style), the Cheka was created by the decree of Vladimir Lenin. These were the beginnings of the Bolsheviks' consolidation of power over their political opponents. The Red Terror was started in September 1918, following a failed assassination attempt on Lenin's life. The Jacobin Terror was an example for the Soviet Bolsheviks. Leon Trotsky had compared Lenin to

Maximilien Robespierre as early as 1904. The Decree on Land ratified the actions of the peasants who throughout Russia gained private land and redistributed it among themselves. The Bolsheviks viewed themselves as representing an alliance of workers and peasants and memorialized that understanding with the Hammer and Sickle on the flag and coat of arms of the Soviet Union. Other decrees: all private property was nationalized; all Russian banks were nationalized; all private bank accounts were expropriated; all the properties of the Church (including bank accounts) were expropriated; all foreign debts were repudiated; control of the factories was given to the soviets; wages were fixed at higher rates than during the war, and a shorter, eight-hour working day was introduced. Bolshevik-led attempts to gain power in other parts of the Russian Empire were largely successful in Russia proper — although the fighting in Moscow lasted for two weeks — but they were less successful in ethnically non-Russian parts of the Empire, which had been clamoring for independence since the February Revolution. For example, the Ukrainian Rada, which had declared autonomy on 23 June 1917, created the Ukrainian People's Republic on 20 November, which was supported by the Ukrainian Congress of Soviets. This led to an armed conflict with the Bolshevik government in Petrograd and, eventually, a Ukrainian declaration of independence from Russia on 25 January 1918. In Estonia, two rival governments emerged: the Estonian Provincial Assembly, established in April 1917, proclaimed itself the supreme legal authority of Estonia on 28 November 1917 and issued the Declaration of Independence on 24 February 1918 Soviet Russia recognized the Executive Committee of the Soviets of Estonia as the legal authority in the province, although the Soviets in Estonia controlled only the capital and a few other major towns The success of the October Revolution transformed the Russian state into a soviet republic. A coalition of anti-Bolshevik groups attempted to unseat the new government in the Russian Civil War from 1918 to 1922.

Something the EZ-directed Wikipedia cautiously hides for her readership, is how Lenin managed to escape from his

Swiss exile and return to Russia in 1917. We therefore turn to a different source: Spartacus.[23]

Prince George Lvov, was appointed the new head of the Provisional Government. One of his first decisions was to allow all political prisoners to return to their homes. Lenin was living in Zurich and he did not hear this news until the 15th March. A group of about twenty Russian exiles arrived at Lenin's home to discuss this important event. Lenin's wife, Nadezhda Krupskaya, explained: "From the moment the news of the February revolution came, Ilyich burned with eagerness to go to Russia. England and France would not for the world have allowed the Bolsheviks to pass through to Russia... As there was no legal way it was necessary to travel illegally. But how?" Aware that the British and French would never allow him a transit visa to Russia through Allied territory in Europe. It was suggested that he should try to return via England under a false passport, but it was decided that this was far too risky and if he was arrested he would be probably interned for the duration of the war. On 19th March 1917 a meeting of

---

23   https://spartacus-educational.com/Lenin_Sealed_Train.htm

socialists was held to discuss the issue. The German socialist Willi Münzenberg was there and later reported that Lenin paced up and down the room declaring, "we must go at all costs". Julius Martov suggested that the best chance would be to send word to the Petrograd Soviet, asking them to offer the Germans repatriation of German prisoners in exchange for the group's safe conduct home via Germany. The Swiss socialist, Robert Grimm, *whom Lenin had described as a "detestable centrist"*,[24] offered to negotiate with the German government in order to obtain a safe passage to Russia. He pointed out that Germany had been spending a great deal of money in producing revolutionary anti-war propaganda in Russia since 1915, in the hope of engineering a withdrawal from the war. This would enable German troops on the Eastern Front to be diverted to the western campaign against Britain and France. Grimm began talks with Count Gisbert von Romberg, the German ambassador in Berne. Alexander Parvus also arrived in Switzerland. The former German Social Democrat who had originally helped to fund Iskra, the Russian revolutionary newspaper, had now

---

24   Oops Lenin, what an abject man you are, for lacking the most elementary self-knowledge

gone over to the German government, operating as an arms contractor and recruiter for the war effort. he had been heavily involved in the German propaganda drive among tsarist troops to destabilize Nicholas II. Parvus made contact with Richard von Kühlmann, a minister at the German Foreign Office. Von Kühlmann sent a message to Army Headquarters explaining the strategy of the German Foreign Office: "The disruption of the Entente and the subsequent creation of political combinations agreeable to us constitute the most important war aim of our diplomacy. Russia appeared to be the weakest link in the enemy chain, the task therefore was gradually to loosen it, and, when possible, to remove it. This was the purpose of the subversive activity we caused to be carried out in Russia behind the front - in the first place promotion of separatist tendencies and support of the Bolsheviks had received a steady flow of funds through various channels and under different labels that they were in a position to be able to build up their main organ, Pravda, to conduct energetic propaganda and appreciably to extend the originally narrow basis of their party." Parvus made contact with General Erich Ludendorff who later admitted his involvement in his autobiography, My War

Memories, 1914-1918 (1920) that he told senior officials: "Our government, in sending Lenin to Russia, took upon itself a tremendous responsibility. From a military point of view his journey was justified, for it was imperative that Russia should fall." General Max Hoffmann, chief of the German General Staff on the Eastern Front commented: "We naturally tried, by means of propaganda, to increase the disintegration that the Russian Revolution had introduced into the Army. Some man at home who had connections with the Russian revolutionaries exiled in Switzerland came upon the idea of employing some of them in order to hasten the undermining and poisoning of the morale of the Russian Army." Hoffmann claims that Reichstag deputy Mathias Erzberger became involved in the negotiations. "And thus it came about that Lenin was conveyed through Germany to Petrograd in the manner that afterwards transpired. In the same way as I send shells into the enemy trenches, as I discharge poison gas at him, I, as an enemy, have the right to employ the expedient of propaganda against his garrisons." Paul Levi, a close associate of Rosa Luxemburg, and a member of the German anti-war Spartacus League, handled the Berne-Zurich end of negotiations, with Karl Radek. Levi was contacted by the German Ambassador in Switzerland and asked: "How can I get in touch with Lenin? I expect final instructions any moment regarding his transportation". Lenin now negotiated the deal with the ambassador that would allow him to travel through Germany. In his farewell message to the Swiss workers Lenin explained his analysis of the situation in Russia. "It has fallen to the lot of the Russian proletariat to begin the series of revolutions whose objective necessity was created by the imperialist world war. We know well that the Russian proletariat is less organized and intellectually less prepared for the task than the working class of other countries... Russia is an agricultural country, one of the most backward of Europe. Socialism cannot be established in Russia immediately. But the peasant character of the development of a democratic-capitalist revolution in Russia and make that a prologue to the world-wide Socialist revolution." Lenin felt he needed the support of other socialists living in Switzerland for his journey through Germany. He sent a telegram to two French anti-war figures living in Switzerland, Romain Rolland and Henri Guilbeaux, asking them to appear in the railroad station on the day of his departure. Rolland refused and sent a message to

Guilbeaux: "If you have any influence on Lenin and his friends, dissuade them from going through Germany. They will cause great damage to the pacifist movement and to themselves, for it will then be said that Zimmerwald is a German child." He then went on to quote Anatoli Lunacharsky who had described Lenin as "a dangerous and cynical adventurer". Lenin insisted that his party of thirty-two should include some twenty non-Bolsheviks, in order to offset the unfavorable impression produced by his trip under German auspices. The people who travelled with him included Gregory Zinoviev, Karl Radek, Inessa Armand, Nadezhda Krupskaya, Georgi Safarov, Zinaida Lilina and Moisey Kharitonov. Lenin's supporters milled around the waiting train carrying revolutionary banners and singing the "Internationale". There was a group of anti-German socialists, shouted, "Spies! German spies! Look how happy they are - going home at the Kaiser's expense!" Anatoli Lunacharsky said that Lenin looked "composed and happy". Willi Münzenberg was there to see Lenin off. He later recalled that as the doors closed Lenin leaned from the carriage window, shook his hand and said, "Either we'll be swinging from the gallows in three months or we shall be in power." At the

German frontier at Gottmadingen station, they were escorted by German soldiers to their own specially commandeered military "sealed train". A locomotive pulled "a green-painted coach comprised of three second-class compartments (mainly for the couples and children) and five third-class compartments, where the single men and women would have to endure the hard wooden seats. *The two German officers escorting them took a compartment at the rear." Once the three of the carriage's four doors at the Russian end were closed shut, Fritz Platten, a Swiss socialist marked them with chalk in German as "sealed". The train was given a high traffic priority by the Germans. Crown Prince Wilhelm, the eldest son of Kaiser Wilhelm II, was delayed for two hours to let Lenin's train to pass. There was a several hours' layover in Berlin during which some members of the German Social Democratic Party boarded the train but were not allowed to communicate with Lenin.* After Germany they travelled through Sweden and Finland. On 2nd April Lenin's family received a telegram: "We arrive Monday at eleven at night. Tell Pravda." Lenin feared being arrested at the Russian border. However, Prince George Lvov's pledge to allow all political prisoners the freedom to return to their homes was kept. At 11.10 at night on 3rd April the train arrived at Finland Station. He was greeted by sailors from the Kronstadt naval base, the Petrograd workers' militia and the Red Guards. As he left the railway station Lenin was lifted on to one of the armored cars specially provided for the occasions. The atmosphere was electric and enthusiastic. Feodosiya Drabkina, who had been an active revolutionary for many years, was in the crowd and later remarked: "Just think, in the course of only a few days Russia had made the transition from the most brutal and cruel arbitrary rule to the freest country in the world." In his speech he announced what became known as the April Theses. Lenin attacked Bolsheviks for supporting the Provisional Government. Instead, he argued, revolutionaries should be telling the people of Russia that they should take over the control of the country. In his speech, Lenin urged the peasants to take the land from the rich landlords and the industrial workers to seize the factories. Lenin accused those Bolsheviks who were still supporting the government of Prince Lvov of betraying socialism and suggested that they should leave the party. Lenin ended his speech by telling the assembled crowd that they must "fight for the social revolution, fight to the end, till the complete victory of the proletariat". Some of the revolutionaries in the crowd rejected Lenin's ideas. Alexander Bogdanov called out that his speech was the "delusion of a lunatic." Joseph Goldenberg, a former of the Bolshevik Central Committee, denounced the views expressed by Lenin: "Everything we have just heard is a complete repudiation of the entire Social Democratic doctrine, of the whole theory of scientific Marxism. We have just heard a clear and unequivocal declaration for anarchism. Its herald, the heir of Bakunin, is Lenin. Lenin the Marxist, Lenin the leader of our fighting Social Democratic Party, is no more. A new Lenin is born, Lenin the anarchist." The journalist, Harold Williams rejected the idea that Lenin could play an important role in affairs: "Lenin, leader of the extreme faction of the Social Democrats, arrived here on Monday night by way of Germany. His action in accepting from the German government a passage from Switzerland through Germany arouses intense indignation here. He has come back breathing fire, and demanding the immediate and unconditional conclusions of peace, civil war against the army and government, and vengeance on Kerensky and Chkheidze, whom he describes as traitors to the cause of International Socialism. At the meeting of Social Democrats yesterday his wild rant was received in dead silence, and he was vigorously attacked, not only by the more moderate Social Democrats, but by members of his own faction. Lenin was left absolutely without supporters. The sharp repulse given to this firebrand was a healthy sign of the growth of practical sense of the Socialist wing, and the generally moderate and sensible tone of the conference of provincial workers' and soldiers' deputies was another hopeful indication of the passing of the revolutionary fever." Albert Rhys Williams, an American visitor to Russia, disagreed with this viewpoint. Williams was convinced that the Bolsheviks would become the new rulers: "The Bolsheviks understood the people. They were strong among the more literate strata, like the sailors, and comprised largely the artisans and laborers of the cities. Sprung directly from the people's lions they spoke the people's language, shared their sorrows and thought their thoughts. They were the people. So they were trusted."

Note that England and France were since long dominated by EZ. Moreover, the fact that Crown Prince Wilhelm, the eldest son of Kaiser Wilhelm II, had to wait two hours to let Lenin's train pass, is direct proof that even the smallest little detail in Lenin's transport had been organized over the heads of both Kaiser Wilhelm II and Tsar Nicholas II, which includes Russia and Germany in the EZ-dominated territories.

The annexation of East-Germany and Poland after World War II by Russia, with Russia representing Bolshevism (and decidedly *not* the Russian people), immediately led to collective blackmail, torture, and loss of freedom in those countries. In 1956, Hungary was smashed under Russian tanks. Please realize that the Russian army just did its job. Had any Russian military, of whatever rank, protested for moral reasons, he would have been shot on the spot, without even the farce of a trial. In 1968, Czechoslovakia's Spring Uprising was again crushed under the wheels of Russian tanks. This, too, was not the *initiative* of the Russian army, but a mandate issued by Stalin. While Eastern Europe was being submitted to Bolshevism, Western Europe was being enslaved by the so-called sexual revolution. EZ's patience goes over centuries. But when time is ripe, they do not wait for one job to be finished, before tackling the next one.

Are these all coincidences, combined with a mega-conspiracy among the governments of more than ten countries? Whosoever believes in such coincidences and conspiracies, is dumb enough to believe in extraterrestrials, UFO's, divination, and communication with the dead, too.

2.2 The Spanish Civil War (1936–1939)

Wikipedia writes on the Red Terror:[25]

> The Red Terror in Spain (Spanish: Terror Rojo) is the name given by some historians to various acts of violence committed from 1936 until the end of the Spanish Civil War "by sections of nearly all the leftist groups". News of the rightist military coup in 1936 unleashed a social revolutionary response, and no republican region escaped revolutionary and anticlerical violence, but it was minimal in the Basque Country. The violence consisted of the killing of tens of thousands of people (including 6,832 members of the Catholic clergy, the vast majority in the summer of 1936 in the wake of the military coup) as well as attacks on landowners, industrialists, and politicians as well as the desecration and burning of monasteries and churches. A process of political polarization had characterized the Spanish Second Republic, and party divisions became increasingly embittered and questions of religious identity came to assume a major political

---

25   https://en.wikipedia.org/wiki/Red_Terror_(Spain)

significance. Electorally, the Church had identified itself with the right, which had set itself against social reform. The failed "pronunciamiento" of 1936 set loose a violent onslaught on those that revolutionaries in the Republican zone identified as enemies; "where the rebellion failed, for several months afterwards merely to be identified as a priest, a religious or simply a militant Christian or member of some apostolic or pious organization, was enough for a person to be executed without trial". In recent years, the Catholic Church has beatified hundreds of the victims, 498 of them on 28 October 2007 in a spectacular ceremony, the largest single number of beatifications in its history. Some estimates of the Red Terror range from 38,000 to ~172,344 lives. Paul Preston, speaking in 2012 at the time of the publication of his book The Spanish Holocaust, put the figure at a little under 50,000. [...]

Others see the persecution and violence as predating the coup and found in what they see as a "radical and antidemocratic" anticlericalism of the Republic and its constitution, with the dissolution of the Jesuits in 1932, the nationalization of virtually all church property in

1933,[26] the prohibition of teaching religion in schools, the prohibition of teaching by clergy and the violent persecution beginning in 1934 in Asturias, with the murder of 37 priests, religious and seminarians and the burning of 58 churches. [...]

According to recent research, some of the Republican death squads were heavily staffed by members of the Soviet Union's secret police, the NKVD. According to author Donald Rayfield, "Stalin, Yezhov, and Beria distrusted Soviet participants in the Spanish war. Military advisors like Vladimir Antonov-Ovseenko, journalists like Koltsov were open to infection by the heresies, especially Trotsky's, prevalent among the Republic's supporters. NKVD agents sent to Spain were therefore keener on abducting and murdering anti-Stalinists among Republican leaders and International Brigade commanders than on fighting Francisco Franco. The defeat of the Republic, in Stalin's eyes, was caused not by the NKVD's diversionary efforts, but by the treachery of the heretics". The most famous member of the Loyalist assassination squads was Erich Mielke, future head of East Germany's

---

26   Exactly the same happened in Lenin's Russia and in Robespierre's France

Stasi. According to Payne, "During the first months of the fighting most of the deaths did not come from combat on the battlefield but from political executions in the rear—the 'Red' and 'White' terrors. The terror consisted of semi-organized actions perpetrated by almost all of the leftist groups, Basque nationalists, largely Catholic but still mostly aligned with the Republicans, being an exception". Payne also contends that unlike the repression by the right, which "was concentrated against the most dangerous opposition elements", the Republican attacks were more irrational, "murdering innocent people and letting some of the more dangerous go free. Moreover, one of the main targets of the Red terror was the clergy, most of whom were not engaged in overt opposition". Describing specifically the Red Terror, Payne states that it "began with the murder of some of the rebels as they attempted to surrender after their revolt had failed in several of the key cities. From there it broadened out to wholesale arrests, and sometimes wholesale executions, of landowners and industrialists, people associated with right-wing groups or the Catholic Church". The Red Terror was "not an irrepressible outpouring of hatred by the man in the street for his 'oppressors,' but a semi-organized activity carried out by sections of nearly all the leftist groups". By contrast, historians such as Helen Graham, Paul Preston, Antony Beevor, Gabriel Jackson, Hugh Thomas, and Ian Gibson have stated that the mass executions behind the Nationalist lines were organized and approved by the Nationalist rebel authorities, and the executions behind the Republican lines were the result of the breakdown of the republican state and the anarchy. That is concurred by Francisco Partaloa, prosecutor of the Madrid High Court of Justice (Tribunal Supremo de Madrid) and Queipo de Llano's friend, who observed repression in both zones. As early as 11 May 1931, when mob violence against the Republic's perceived enemies had led to the burning of churches, convents, and religious schools, the Church had sometimes been seen as the ally of the authoritarian right. The academic Mary Vincent has written: "There was no doubt that the Church would line up with the rebels against the Republic. The Jesuit priests of the city of Salamanca were among the first volunteers to present themselves to the military authorities.... The tragedy of the Second Republic was that it abetted its own destruction; the tragedy of the

Church was that it became so closely allied with its self-styled defenders". During the war, the nationalists claimed that 20,000 priests had been killed; the figure is now put at 4,184 priests, 2,365 members of other religious institutes and 283 nuns, the vast majority during the summer of 1936. Payne has called the terror the "most extensive and violent persecution of Catholicism in Western History, in some way even more intense than that of the French Revolution", driving Catholics, left with little alternative, to the Nationalists even more than would have been expected to do so. Figures for the Red Terror range from 38,000 to 172,344. Historian Beevor "reckons Franco's ensuing 'white terror' claimed 200,000 lives. The 'red terror' had already killed 38,000." According to Julio de la Cueva, the toll of the Red Terror was 72,344 lives. Hugh Thomas and Paul Preston said that the death toll was 55,000, and Spanish historian Julian Casanova said that the death toll was fewer than 60,000. Previously, Payne had suggested, "The toll taken by the respective terrors may never be known exactly. The left slaughtered more in the first months, but the Nationalist repression probably reached its height only after the war had ended, when punishment was exacted and vengeance wreaked on the vanquished left. The White Terror may have slain 50,000, perhaps fewer, during the war. The Franco government now gives the names of 61,000 victims of the Red Terror, but this is not subject to objective verification. The number of victims of the Nationalist repression, during and after the war, was undoubtedly greater than that". In "Checas de Madrid", journalist and historian César Vidal comes to a nationwide total of 110,965 victims of Republican repression; 11,705 people being killed in Madrid alone. Historian Santos Juliá, in the work "Víctimas de la Guerra Civil" provides approximate figures: about 50,000 victims of the Republican repression; about 100,000 victims of the Francoist repression during the war with some 40,000 after the war.

Even today, Red Spain does not admit the relevance of these historical facts. It shows how intensely the EZ-bolshevists managed to brainwash it. No doubt, the Church representatives in pre-war Spain had too openly sympathized with the wealthy. No doubt, that needed rectification. However, the five historical events

(i)   the gratuity of dissolving the Jesuits in 1932;

(ii)   the confiscation of all Church property, without a due process;

(iii)   the gratuity of prohibiting teaching of Catholic Doctrine at high schools;

(iv)   the gratuity of prohibiting clergy to teach in private Catholic schools;

(v)   the violent anti-Catholic persecution in Asturias in 1934 (two years before the war);

all were a clear warning to the Catholics, that, without due response, they would be roasted alive. So why did nobody wake up in Spain? Simply, because Spaniards are still proud, to date, of their descent from the greatest Empire ever on this planet. They are equally proud to the left as to the right. And for such an Empire, there simply exists *nothing* outside it. All problems always start from within, and are to be directly eliminated from within. Hence, Catholic right (give me a puking bag) was nowhere close to imagining what enemy they were dealing with. They had no idea that, whatever the outcome of the fratricide Spanish Civil War, would perpetuate a deep chasm through Spanish society, just like EZ managed to do time and again in history, starting from that day in Ancient Greece.

Note that el Caudillo or "el generalísimo" Francisco Franco did not like intervening militarily. When he was put in charge of the African legions, he had actually no choice, as the legions had already upraised.

Now, who could tell me the name of a single Spaniard in 1930, either Catholic or Republican, who was willing to provoke an irrationally deep hatred between two different ideologies that had hitherto lived peacefully together? The answer is oh so simple: there was none. Spanish are fighters but not suicide commando's: deep hatred was certainly not going to make life easier in Spain, neither for Catholics, nor for Republicans.

Only EZ was interested in ripping Spain apart into two parts at permanent war. How much easier can you get hold of a country when it is deeply divided and involved in a horrible fraternal war, than when it is united?[27]

Franco's army came to the rescue of defenseless Catholics, and in doing so it had no choice but crashing the Bolshevik uprising militarily. But it was already too late. Many Spanish traditional socialists and communists had been purged by EZ and replaced by extremist nuts, who really belonged either in prison or in a nut house. By 1939, the Spanish population had suffered so many losses at both sides, that not a single Spaniard (except Escrivà himself) was able to extinguish the deep hatred in his heart.

Exactly the same mentality blindfolded Spain with respect to the 2004 terror attack in Madrid-Atocha (train station). It was a piece of cake for EZ, who know the ins and outs of *both* Spanish politics (how to play out

---

27   The Christ loosely quoted the Old Testament when saying to some malicious Jews "Every kingdom divided against itself is brought to desolation, and every city or house divided against itself will not stand" (Matthew 12:25).

Catholics against Republicans) *and* Spanish secret services: not long before 2004, José María Aznar had asked CIA's help for ending the terror by a group of EZ-driven, Bask retards, called ETA. This Bask terror group was historically schooled by Jesuits, whose frequent expulsions and/or dissolutions in history make one think "mafia". I do not exclude, a priori, the possibility that Jesuits were since long (many centuries) deeply penetrated by EZ. Too bad, the Spanish pride of stemming from the largest empire of this planet blinds them to such extent that they rather believe utter crap[28] concerning the 2004 terror attack, than allowing for the existence of an exterior Jewish mafia which is 50 times the Spanish economic size.

2.3 The Italian Risorgimento (1815–1871–1918)

Napoleon's conquests spread EZ-inspired (in Europe known as "Republican") ideas throughout Europe. His Austerlitz victory ended the Habsburg rule over most of Italy. The Italian peninsular territories, which escaped to Napoleon's conquests, were called "terre irredente" (non-

---

28 Some speak of Al Qaeda, not knowing that it is a mere weapon under full EZ control; others speak of "isolated pockets of terrorists", and some even speak of the Moroccan secret services! It is outrageously dumb, because none of these options can explain how all trains evaporated overnight, except a few parts that were chemically treated to the point of leaving no single trace of the explosives used.

liberated territories) by the Italian Republicans. Note for the non-Italian reader: *Piedmont* is the State with Turin as capital (the North-West of present-day Italy). Wikipedia writes:[29]

> The Italian Risorgimento (Resurgence) was the political and social movement that consolidated different states of the Italian peninsula into the single state of the Kingdom of Italy in the 19th century. The process began in 1815 with the Congress of Vienna and was completed in 1871 when Rome became the capital of the Kingdom of Italy. The term, which also designates the cultural, political and social movement that promoted unification, recalls the romantic, nationalist and patriotic ideals of an Italian renaissance through the conquest of a unified political identity that, by sinking its ancient roots during the Roman period, "suffered an abrupt halt [or loss] of its political unity in 476 AD after the collapse of the West Roman Empire". However, some of the "terre irredente" did not join the Kingdom of Italy until 1918 after Italy defeated Austria-Hungary in World War I. For this reason, sometimes the period is extended to include the

---

29   https://en.wikipedia.org/wiki/Italian_unification

late 19th-century and the First World War (1915–1918), until the 4 November 1918 Armistice of Villa Giusti, which is considered the completion of unification. This view is followed, for example, at the Central Museum of Risorgimento at the Vittoriano. Historians continue to debate many of the key features and personalities of the movement. After Napoleon fell, the Congress of Vienna (1814–15) restored the pre-Napoleonic patchwork of independent governments. Italy was again controlled largely by the Austrian Empire and the Habsburgs, as they directly controlled the predominantly Italian-speaking northeastern part of Italy and were, together, the most powerful force against unification. [...] Exiles dreamed of unification. Three ideals of unification appeared. Vincenzo Gioberti, a Piedmontese priest, had suggested a confederation of Italian states under leadership of the Pope in his 1842 book, Of the Moral and Civil Primacy of the Italians. Pope Pius IX at first appeared interested but he turned reactionary and led the battle against liberalism and nationalism.

It seems that Pope Pius IX (or his close collaborators) smelled the EZ-background, or at least, the freemasonic orientation of the Risorgimento.

Giuseppe Mazzini and Carlo Cattaneo wanted the unification of Italy under a federal republic, which proved too extreme for most nationalists. The middle position was proposed by Cesare Balbo (1789-1853) as a confederation of separate Italian states led by Piedmont. One of the most influential revolutionary groups was the "Carboneria", a secret political discussion group formed in Southern Italy early in the 19th century; the members were called Carbonari. After 1815, Freemasonry in Italy was repressed and discredited due to its French connections. A void was left that the Carboneria filled with a movement that closely resembled Freemasonry but with a commitment to Italian nationalism and no association with Napoleon and his government. The response came from middle class professionals and business men and some intellectuals. The Carboneria disowned Napoleon but nevertheless were inspired by the principles of the French Revolution regarding liberty, equality and fraternity. They developed their own rituals, and were strongly anticlerical. The

Carboneria movement spread across Italy. Conservative governments feared the Carboneria, imposing stiff penalties on men discovered to be members. Nevertheless, the movement survived and continued to be a source of political turmoil in Italy from 1820 until after unification. The Carbonari condemned Napoleon III (who, as a young man, had fought on the side of the Carbonari) to death for failing to unite Italy, and the group almost succeeded in assassinating him in 1858, when Felice Orsini, Giovanni Andrea Pieri, Carlo Di Rudio and Andrea Gomez launched three bombs at him. Many leaders of the unification movement were at one time or other members of this organization. The chief purpose was to defeat tyranny [read: Austrian rule and the Pope's religious influence] and to establish "constitutional" government. Though contributing some service to the cause of Italian unity, historians such as Cornelia Shiver doubt that their achievements were proportional to their pretensions. Many leading Carbonari revolutionaries wanted a republic, two of the most prominent being Giuseppe Mazzini and Giuseppe Garibaldi. Mazzini's activity in revolutionary movements caused him to be imprisoned soon after he joined. While in prison, he concluded that Italy could – and therefore should – be unified, and he formulated a program for establishing a free, independent, and republican nation with Rome as its capital. Following his release in 1831, he went to Marseille in France, where he organized a new political society called "La Giovane Italia" (Young Italy), whose motto was "Dio e Popolo" (God and People), which sought the unification of Italy. Garibaldi, a native of Nice (then part of Piedmont), participated in an uprising in Piedmont in 1834 and was sentenced to death. He escaped to South America, though, spending fourteen years in exile, taking part in several wars, and learning the art of guerrilla warfare before his return to Italy in 1848. In 1820, Spaniards successfully revolted over disputes about their Constitution, which influenced the development of a similar movement in Italy. Inspired by the Spaniards (who, in 1812, had created their constitution), a regiment in the army of the Kingdom of Two Sicilies, commanded by Guglielmo Pepe, a "Carbonaro" (member of the secret republican organization), mutinied, conquering the peninsular part of Two Sicilies. The king, Ferdinand I, agreed to enact a new constitution. The revolutionaries, though, failed to court popular support and fell to Austrian troops of the Holy Alliance. Ferdinand abolished the constitution and began systematically persecuting known revolutionaries. Many supporters of revolution in Sicily, including the scholar Michele Amari, were forced into exile during the decades that followed.

The leader of the 1821 revolutionary movement in Piedmont was Santorre di Santarosa, who wanted to remove the Austrians and unify Italy under the House of Savoy. The Piedmont revolt started in Alessandria, where troops adopted the green, white, and red tricolore of the Cisalpine Republic. The king's regent, prince Charles Albert, acting while the king Charles Felix was away, approved a new constitution to appease the revolutionaries, but when the king returned he disavowed the constitution and requested assistance from the Holy Alliance. Di Santarosa's troops were defeated, and the would-be Piedmontese revolutionary fled to Paris. In Milan, Silvio Pellico and Pietro Maroncelli organized several attempts to weaken the hold of the Austrian "despotism" by indirect educational means. In October 1820, Pellico and Maroncelli were arrested on the charge of carbonarism and imprisoned. Historian Denis Mack Smith argues:

"Few people in 1830, believed that an Italian nation might exist. There were eight states in the peninsula, each with distinct laws and traditions. No one had had the desire or the resources to revive Napoleon's partial experiment in unification. The settlement of 1814-15, had merely restored regional divisions, with the added disadvantage that the decisive victory of Austria over France temporarily hindered Italians in playing off their former oppressors against each other. ... Italians who, like Ugo Foscolo and Gabriele Rossetti, harbored patriotic sentiments, were driven into exile. The largest Italian state, the Bourbon Kingdom of the Two Sicilies, with its 8 million inhabitants, seemed aloof and indifferent: Sicily and Naples had once formed part of Spain, and it had always been foreign to the rest of Italy. The common people in each region, and even the intellectual elite, spoke their mutually unintelligible dialects, and lacked the least vestiges of national consciousness. They wanted good government, not self-government, and had welcomed Napoleon and the French as more equitable and efficient than their native dynasties." After 1830, revolutionary sentiment in favor of a unified Italy began to experience a resurgence, and a series of insurrections laid the groundwork for the creation of one nation along the Italian peninsula. The Duke of Modena, Francis IV, was an ambitious noble, and he hoped to become king of Northern Italy by increasing his territory. In 1826, Francis made it clear that he would not act against those who subverted opposition toward the unification of Italy. Encouraged by the declaration, revolutionaries in the region began to organize. During the July Revolution of 1830 in France, revolutionaries forced the king to abdicate and created the July Monarchy with encouragement from the new French king, Louis-Philippe. Louis-Philippe had promised revolutionaries such as Ciro Menotti that he would intervene if Austria tried to interfere in Italy with troops. Fearing he would lose his throne, Louis-Philippe did not, however, intervene in Menotti's planned uprising. The Duke of Modena abandoned his Carbonari supporters, arrested Menotti and other conspirators in 1831, and once again conquered his duchy with help from the Austrian troops. Menotti was executed, and the idea of a revolution centered in Modena faded. At the same time, other insurrections arose in the Papal Legations of Bologna, Ferrara, Ravenna, Forlì, Ancona and Perugia. These successful revolutions, which adopted the tricolor in favor of the Papal flag, quickly spread to cover all the Papal Legations, and their newly installed local governments proclaimed the creation of a united Italian nation. The revolts in Modena and the Papal Legations inspired similar activity in the Duchy of Parma, where the tricolor flag was adopted. The Parmesan Duchess Marie Louise left the city during the political upheaval. Insurrected provinces planned to unite as the "Provincie Italiane unite" (United Italian Provinces), which prompted Pope Gregory XVI to ask for Austrian help against the rebels. Austrian Chancellor Metternich warned Louis-Philippe that Austria had no intention of letting Italian matters be, and that French intervention would not be tolerated. Louis-Philippe withheld any military help and even arrested Italian patriots living in France. In early 1831, the Austrian army began its march across the Italian peninsula, slowly crushing resistance in each province that had revolted. This military action suppressed much of the fledgling revolutionary movement, and resulted in the arrest of many radical leaders. Initially, Pius IX had been something of a reformer, but conflicts with the revolutionaries soured him on the idea of constitutional government. In November 1848, following the assassination of his Minister Pellegrino Rossi, Pius IX fled just before Giuseppe Garibaldi and other patriots arrived in Rome. In early 1849, elections were held for a Constituent Assembly, which proclaimed a Roman Republic on 9 February. On 2 February 1849, at a political rally held in the Apollo Theater, a young Roman priest, the Abbé Carlo Arduini, had made a speech in which he had declared that the temporal power of the popes was a "historical lie, a political imposture, and a religious immorality". In early March 1849, Giuseppe Mazzini arrived in Rome and was appointed Chief Minister. In the Constitution of the Roman Republic, religious freedom was guaranteed by article 7, the independence of the pope as head of the Catholic Church was guaranteed by article 8 of the "Principi fondamentali", while the death penalty was abolished by article 5, and free public education was provided by article 8 of the Titolo I. Daniele Manin and Niccolò Tommaseo after the proclamation of the Republic of San Marco. Before the powers could respond to the founding of the Roman Republic, Charles Albert, whose army had been trained by the exiled Polish general Albert Chrzanowski, renewed the war with Austria. He was quickly defeated by Radetzky at Novara on 23 March 1849. Charles Albert abdicated in favor of his son, Victor Emmanuel II, and Piedmontese ambitions to unite Italy or conquer Lombardy were, for the moment, brought to an end. The war ended with a treaty signed on 9 August. A popular revolt broke out in Brescia on the same day as the defeat at Novara, but was suppressed by the Austrians ten days later. There remained the Roman and Venetian Republics. In April, a French force under Charles Oudinot was sent to Rome. Apparently, the French first wished to mediate between the Pope and his subjects, but soon the French were determined to restore the Pope. After a two-month siege, Rome capitulated on 29 June 1849 and the Pope was restored. Garibaldi and Mazzini once again fled into exile—in 1850 Garibaldi went to New York City. Meanwhile, the Austrians besieged Venice, which defended by a volunteer army led by Daniele Manin and Guglielmo Pepe, who were forced to surrender on 24 August. Pro-independence fighters were hanged "en masse" in Belfiore, while the Austrians moved to restore order in central Italy, restoring the princes who had been expelled and establishing their control over the Papal

Legations. The revolutions were thus completely crushed.

This is very important: Garibaldi chose New York City, EZ's capital, as his exile. This leaves little doubt that Garibaldi was an EZ-puppet. Italian unification was a successful EZ-directed enterprise to end the Austrian supremacy. This supremacy is often described as "tyrannical", though in comparison with EZ-founded Gestapo-communism, it was an Eden's garden of freedom and peace. Moreover, the age-old French EZ-role, in fighting Catholic countries (like the Austrian Empire), clearly shows the snake sliming from France, southward to Italy. And what remains of Italian unification today? A very deep enmity between an embittered North (with respect to the river Pò) and the mafia-controlled South (with respect to Rome). EZ again triumphed on all accounts.

2.4 The French Civil War (1789–1798)

Wikipedia writes about the French Revolution:[30]

Freemasonry played an important role in the revolution. Originally largely apolitical,

---

30   https://en.wikipedia.org/wiki/French_Revolution

Freemasonry was radicalized in the late 18th century through the introduction of higher grades, which emphasized themes of liberty, equality, and fraternity. Virtually every major player in the Revolution was a Freemason and these themes became the widely recognized slogan of the revolution.

Freemasonry was radicalized by the introduction of higher grades? This Wiki-writer, most probably a Freemason himself, has no clue about wars for power, let alone history. The radicalization was nothing but a reflection of the slow penetration of EZ into most freemason lodges, a penetration that most Freemasons were too ingenuous to realize. The quote goes on:

In 1774 Louis XVI ascended to the throne in the middle of a financial crisis in which the state was faced with a budget deficit and was nearing bankruptcy. This was due in part to France's costly involvements in the Seven Years' War and later the American Revolutionary War. In May 1776, finance minister Turgot was dismissed, after failing to enact reforms. The next year, Jacques Necker, a foreigner, was appointed Comptroller-General of Finance. He could not be made an official minister because he was a

Protestant. Necker realized that the country's extremely regressive tax system subjected the lower classes to a heavy burden, while numerous exemptions existed for the nobility and clergy. He argued that the country could not be taxed higher; that tax exemptions for the nobility and clergy must be reduced; and proposed that borrowing more money would solve the country's fiscal shortages. Necker published a report to support this claim that underestimated the deficit by roughly 36 million livres, and proposed restricting the power of the parliaments. This was not received well by the King's ministers, and Necker, hoping to bolster his position, argued to be made a minister. The King refused, Necker was dismissed, and Charles Alexandre de Calonne was appointed to the Comptrollership. Calonne initially spent liberally, but he quickly realized the critical financial situation and proposed a new tax code. The proposal included a consistent land tax, which would include taxation of the nobility and clergy. Faced with opposition from the "parlements", Calonne organized the summoning of the Assembly of Notables. But the Assembly failed to endorse Calonne's proposals and instead weakened his position through its criticism. In response, the King announced the calling of the

Estates-General for May 1789, the first time the body had been summoned since 1614. This was a signal that the Bourbon monarchy was in a weakened state and subject to the demands of its people.

The Estates-General was organized into three estates: the clergy, the nobility, and the rest of France. It had last met in 1614. Elections were held in the spring of 1789; suffrage requirements for the Third Estate were for French-born or naturalized males, aged 25 years or more, who resided where the vote was to take place and who paid taxes. Strong turnout produced 1,201 delegates, including 303 clergymen, 291 nobles and 610 members of the Third Estate. The First Estate represented 100,000 Catholic clergy; the Church owned about 10% of the land and collected its own taxes (the tithe) on peasants. The lands were controlled by bishops and abbots of monasteries, but two-thirds of the 303 delegates from the First Estate were ordinary parish priests; only 51 were bishops. The Second Estate represented the nobility, about 400,000 men and women who owned about 25% of the land and collected seigneurial dues and rents from their peasant tenants. About a third of these deputies were nobles, mostly with minor holdings. The Third Estate representation was doubled to 610 men, representing 95% of the population. Half were well educated lawyers or local officials. Nearly a third were in trades or industry; 51 were wealthy land owners. To assist delegates, "Books of grievances" (cahiers de doléances) were compiled to list problems. The books articulated ideas which would have seemed radical only months before; however, most supported the monarchical system in general. Many assumed the Estates-General would approve future taxes, and Enlightenment ideals were relatively rare. Pamphlets by liberal nobles and clergy became widespread after the lifting of press censorship. The Abbé Sieyès, a theorist and Catholic clergyman, argued the paramount importance of the Third Estate in the pamphlet "Qu'est-ce que le tiers état"? (What is the Third Estate?) published in January, 1789. He asserted: "What is the Third Estate? Everything. What has it been until now in the political order? Nothing. What does it want to be? Something." The Estates-General convened in the Grands Salles des Menus-Plaisirs in Versailles on 5 May 1789 and opened with a three-hour speech by Necker. The Third Estate demanded that the credentials of deputies should be verified by all deputies, rather than each estate verifying the credentials of its own members, but negotiations with the other estates failed to achieve this. The commoners appealed to the clergy, who asked for more time. Necker then stated that each estate should verify its own members' credentials and that the king should act as arbitrator. The middle class were the ones who fanned the flames of revolution. They established the National Assembly and tried to pressure the aristocracy to spread their money evenly between the upper, middle and lower classes. On 10 June 1789 Abbé Sieyès moved that the Third Estate, now meeting as the Communes (English: "Commons") proceed with verifying its own powers and invite the other two estates to take part, but not to wait for them. They proceeded to do so two days later, completing the process on 17 June. Then they voted a measure far more radical, declaring themselves the National Assembly, an assembly not of the Estates but of "the People". They invited the other orders to join them, but made it clear they intended to conduct the nation's affairs with or without them. In an attempt to keep control of the process and prevent the Assembly from convening, Louis XVI ordered the closure of the Salle des États where the Assembly met, making an excuse that the carpenters needed to prepare the hall for a royal speech in two days. Weather did not allow an outdoor meeting, and fearing an attack ordered by Louis XVI, they met in a tennis court just outside Versailles, where they proceeded to swear the Tennis Court Oath (20 June 1789) under which they agreed not to separate until they had given France a constitution. A majority of the representatives of the clergy soon joined them, as did 47 members of the nobility. By 27 June, the royal party had overtly given in, although the military began to arrive in large numbers around Paris and Versailles. Messages of support for the Assembly poured in from Paris and other French cities. By this time, Necker had earned the enmity of many members of the French court for his overt manipulation of public opinion. Marie Antoinette, the King's younger brother the Comte d'Artois, and other conservative members of the King's privy council urged him to dismiss Necker as financial advisor. On 11 July 1789, after Necker published an inaccurate account of the government's debts and made it available to the public, the King fired him, and completely restructured the finance ministry at the same time. Many Parisians presumed Louis' actions to be aimed against the Assembly and began open rebellion when they heard the news the next day. They were also afraid that arriving soldiers – mostly foreign mercenaries – had been summoned to shut down the National Constituent Assembly. The Assembly, meeting at Versailles, went into nonstop session to prevent another eviction from their meeting place. Paris was soon consumed by riots, chaos, and widespread looting. The mobs soon had the support of some of the French Guard, who were armed and trained soldiers. On 14 July, the insurgents set their eyes on the large weapons and ammunition cache inside the Bastille fortress, which was also perceived to be a symbol of royal power. After several hours of combat, the prison fell that afternoon. Despite ordering a ceasefire, which prevented a mutual massacre, Governor Marquis Bernard-René de Launay was beaten, stabbed and decapitated; his head was placed on a pike and paraded about the city. Although the fortress had held only seven prisoners (four forgers, two noblemen kept for immoral behavior, and a murder suspect) the Bastille served as a potent symbol of everything hated under the Ancien Régime. Returning to the

Hôtel de Ville (city hall), the mob accused the prévôt des marchands (roughly, mayor) Jacques de Flesselles of treachery and butchered him. The King, alarmed by the violence, backed down, at least for the time being. The Marquis de Lafayette took up command of the National Guard at Paris. Jean-Sylvain Bailly, president of the Assembly at the time of the Tennis Court Oath, became the city's mayor under a new governmental structure known as the commune. The King visited Paris, where, on 17 July he accepted a tricolored cockade, to cries of Vive la Nation ("Long live the Nation") and Vive le Roi ("Long live the King"). Necker was recalled to power, but his triumph was short-lived. An astute financier but a less astute politician, Necker overplayed his hand by demanding and obtaining a general amnesty, losing much of the people's favor. As civil authority rapidly deteriorated, with random acts of violence and theft breaking out across the country, members of the nobility, fearing for their safety, fled to neighboring countries; many of these émigrés, as they were called, funded counter-revolutionary causes within France and urged foreign monarchs to offer military support to a counter-revolution. By late July, the spirit of popular sovereignty had spread throughout France. In rural areas, many commoners began to form militias and arm themselves against a foreign invasion: some attacked the châteaux of the nobility as part of a general agrarian insurrection known as "la Grande Peur" ("the Great Fear"). In addition, wild rumors and paranoia caused widespread unrest and civil disturbances that contributed to the collapse of law and order.

Somewhere in this long quote one may read:

"The middle class were the ones who fanned the flames of revolution. They established the National Assembly and tried to pressure the aristocracy to spread their money evenly between the upper, middle and lower classes."

Middle class? Again a freemasonic confusion of concepts. The Middle class was virtually inexistent at that time. The ones who fanned the flames of revolution, like always in modern history, were *exclusively* EZ-agitators. They are so easily recognizable because they are the only ones who want create chaos. *Western ideologues (e.g. Karl Marx) might shout out for popular insurrection, but always aim to achieving an, in their eyes, positive goal for society.*

What is unique to EZ, is that they only seek chaos and destruction.

An idea that always appeals to the large majority of a well-run nation is that of communism. That appeal is merely egotistical. "I get more money, by *legally* impoverishing others, albeit *immorally*." Moreover, the duration of such appeal is very short-lived. Actually, not because anything is wrong with the social aspect of communism,[31] but because of its abject intolerance it always gives birth to.

The Wikipedia author continues:

> During the Reign of Terror, extreme efforts of de-Christianisation ensued, including the imprisonment and massacre of priests and destruction of churches and religious images throughout France. An effort was made to replace the Catholic Church altogether, with civic festivals replacing religious ones. The establishment of the Cult of Reason was the final step of radical de-Christianization. These events led to a widespread disillusionment with the Revolution and to counter-rebellions across France. Locals often resisted de-Christianization by attacking revolutionary agents and hiding

---

31   As a Christian I am well aware that "social communism" was adopted by Petrus' Church.

members of the clergy who were being hunted. Eventually, Robespierre and the Committee of Public Safety were forced to denounce the campaign, replacing the Cult of Reason with the deist but still non-Christian Cult of the Supreme Being. The Concordat of 1801 between Napoleon and the Church ended the de-Christianization period and established the rules for a relationship between the Catholic Church and the French State that lasted until it was abrogated by the Third Republic via the separation of church and state on 11 December 1905. The persecution of the Church led to a counter-revolution known as the Revolt in the Vendée. [...] Some historians claim that after that Vendéan defeat Convention Republic armies in 1794 massacred 117,000 Vendéan civilians to obliterate the Vendéan people, but others contest that claim. Some historians consider the total civil war to have lasted until 1796 with a toll of 170,000 or 450,000 lives. Because of the extremely brutal forms that the Republican repression took in many places, historians such as Reynald Secher have called the event a "genocide". Historian François Furet concluded that the repression in the Vendee "not only revealed massacre and destruction on an unprecedented scale but also a zeal so violent that it has bestowed as its legacy much of the region's identity."

Apparently, the French Revolution needed a genocide to maintain power, just like the Russian. Another typical characteristic of EZ-led revolutions. Probably, this is the reason that Turks are fundamentally unable to take their responsibility for exterminating the Armenian Turks (some 4,000,000 people). I guess, someway, they instinctively feel no Turk would ever decide such a brutal thing. But the evidence is overwhelming. Hence, the only way for the Turks to escape the genocidal blame on their National Flag, is to charge EZ-agitators for it. The big Turkish problem is that they have no idea of EZ altogether.

Not everything is bad that comes from France, though, even after their prostration to communism in 1789, to militarism shortly thereafter, and finally to intolerant republicanism. For example, on Friday, January 9th, in the year 2015, Président François Hollande declared on national television about Charlie Hebdo: "Ceux qui ont commis ces actes: ces terroristes, ces illuminés, ces fanatiques, n'ont rien à voir avec la religion Musulmane". Translated, this becomes "Those who committed these acts: these terrorists, these illuminati, these fanatics, have nothing whatsoever to do with the Muslim religion".

This is absolutely true, and EZ will never forgive him for declaring this so openly. Although the Muslim religion does incite to violence of whatever kind, *in the case of Charlie Hebdo every single move was directed by EZ, and by the EZ-controlled National French Security; if any Muslims were implicated, that was only as lowest-level mercenaries or victims.*

2.5 The American Civil War (1861–1865)

The snake continued its triumphant journey and decided to cross the Atlantic. Everything was prepared in the EZ-headquarters of New York. A little instigation got the northerners so far as to start a war on the south. This deeply cut the American country into two parts. This time, EZ would use southern slavery in order to brainwash the northerners.[32] However, after the war, America was not divided enough for EZ to be able to govern with virtually no opposition. Wikipedia writes the following: [33]

> Slavery was a major cause of disunion. Although there were opposing views even in the Union States, most northern soldiers were mostly indifferent on the subject of slavery, while

---

32   I abhor of slavery. I only doubt a Civil War was the most intelligent and morally responsible way to get rid of it.

33   https://en.wikipedia.org/wiki/American_Civil_War

Confederates fought the war mainly to protect a southern society of which slavery was an integral part. From the anti-slavery perspective, the issue was primarily about whether the system of slavery was an anachronistic evil that was incompatible with republicanism. The strategy of the anti-slavery forces was containment—to stop the expansion and thus put slavery on a path to gradual extinction. The slave-holding interests in the South denounced this strategy as infringing upon their Constitutional rights. Southern whites believed that the emancipation of slaves would destroy the South's economy, due to the large amount of capital invested in slaves and fears of integrating the ex-slave black population. In particular, southerners feared a repeat of "the horrors of Santo Domingo", in which nearly all white people – including men, women, children, and even many sympathetic to abolition – were killed after the successful slave revolt in Haiti. Historian Thomas Fleming points to the historical phrase "a disease in the public mind" used by critics of this idea, and proposes it contributed to the segregation in the Jim Crow era following emancipation. These fears were exacerbated by the recent attempts of John Brown to instigate an armed slave rebellion in the South.

It is somewhat funny to read, in two adjacent sentences, that "slavery was a major cause of disunion", and "most northern soldiers were mostly indifferent on the subject of slavery". Do I have to deduce that soldiers had a different average opinion on slavery than the rest of the people? I think it is plain crap. The whole idea to end slavery by a war was not American in the first place. And for sure, John Brown got well paid by EZ for his most welcome services.

Wikipedia continues with the United States National Park Service's figures in its official tally of war losses, about 900,000 for both the Union and the Confederacy, summing to 1,800,000 in total. This is a sordid caricature of a clever, political, agreement on the abolishment of slavery.

Have any diplomatic approaches preceded the unilaterally declared war? Did the North offer the South a financial compensation for their loss of social stability? Did the North try to buy out Southern slaves, with a granted schooling program in the North? The sordid reality is that neither North nor South gave a damn about black slavery. It was a mere financial war. Now, who would be interested in that?

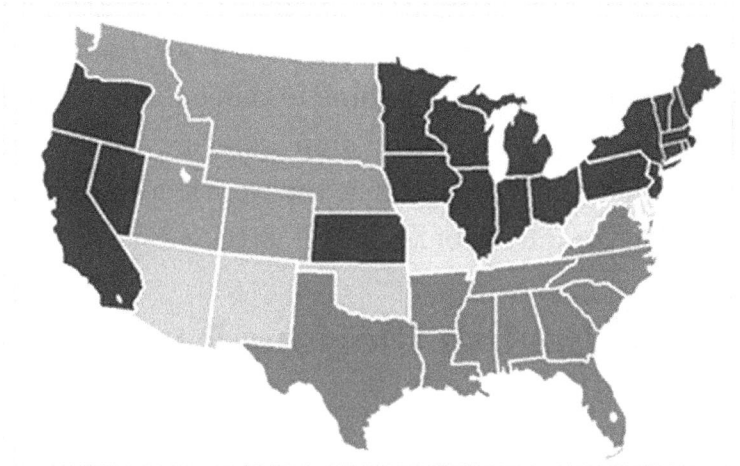

US Secession map 1863. The Union vs. the
Confederacy.

■ Union states

■ Union territories not permitting slavery

□ Border Union states, permitting slavery

(One of these states, West Virginia was created in
1863)

■ Confederate states

■ Union territories that permitted slavery

(claimed by Confederacy) at the start of the war,
but where slavery was outlawed in 1862

Who would provide financial loans to both sides, and increase their patrimony by collecting the outrageous interest rates? Maybe something to think about, my dear Americans. And for sure, stop carrying along that German-like guilt complex that you were somehow guilty of starting the war, or of keeping it alive so long.

2.6 The English Glorious Revolution (1688)

After the bloody English Civil War (1642–1651) another Revolution quickly followed, to complete EZ's dominion over England. Wikipedia reports:[34]

> The Glorious Revolution, also called the Revolution of 1688, was the overthrow of King James II of England (James VII of Scotland) by a union of English Parliamentarians with the Dutch stadtholder William III, Prince of Orange, who was James's nephew and son-in-law. William's successful invasion of England with a Dutch fleet and army led to his ascension to the throne as William III of England jointly with his wife, Mary II, James's daughter, after the Declaration of Right, leading to the Bill of Rights 1689. King James's policies of religious tolerance

---

34   https://en.wikipedia.org/wiki/Glorious_Revolution

after 1685 met with increasing opposition from members of leading political circles, who were troubled by the King's Catholicism and his close ties with France. The crisis facing the King came to a head in 1688, with the birth of his son, James, on 10 June (Julian calendar). This changed the existing line of succession by displacing the heir presumptive (his 26-year-old daughter Mary, a Protestant and the wife of William of Orange) with young James as heir apparent. The establishment of a Roman Catholic dynasty in the kingdoms now seemed likely. Some Tory members of parliament worked with members of the opposition Whigs in an attempt to resolve the crisis by secretly initiating dialogue with William of Orange to come to England, outside the jurisdiction of the English Parliament. Stadtholder William, the de facto head of state of the Dutch United Provinces, feared a Catholic Anglo–French alliance and had already been planning a military intervention in England. After consolidating political and financial support, William crossed the North Sea and English Channel with a large invasion fleet in November 1688, landing at Torbay. After only two minor clashes between the two opposing armies in England, and anti-Catholic riots in several towns,

James's regime collapsed, largely because of a lack of resolve shown by the king. This was followed, however, by the protracted Williamite War in Ireland and Dundee's rising in Scotland. In England's distant American colonies, the revolution led to the collapse of the Dominion of New England and the overthrow of the Province of Maryland's government. Following a defeat of his forces at the Battle of Reading on 9 December, James and his wife Mary fled England; James, however, returned to London for a two-week period that culminated in his final departure for France on 23 December. By threatening to withdraw his troops, William in February 1689 (New Style Julian calendar) convinced a newly chosen Convention Parliament to make him and his wife joint monarchs. The Revolution permanently ended any chance of Catholicism becoming re-established in England. For British Catholics its effects were disastrous both socially and politically: For over a century Catholics were denied the right to vote and sit in the Westminster Parliament; they were also denied commissions in the army, and the monarch was forbidden to be Catholic or to marry a Catholic, this latter prohibition remaining in force until 2015. The Revolution led to limited tolerance for

Nonconformist Protestants, although it would be some time before they had full political rights. It has been argued, mainly by Whig historians, that James's overthrow began modern English parliamentary democracy: The Bill of Rights 1689 has become one of the most important documents in the political history of Britain and never since has the monarch held absolute power. Internationally, the Revolution was related to the War of the Grand Alliance on mainland Europe. It has been seen as the last successful invasion of England. It ended all attempts by England in the Anglo-Dutch Wars of the 17th century to subdue the Dutch Republic by military force. The resulting economic integration and military co-operation between the English and Dutch navies, however, shifted the dominance in world trade from the Dutch Republic to England and later to Great Britain. The expression "Glorious Revolution" was first used by John Hampden in late 1689, and is an expression that is still used by the British Parliament. The Glorious Revolution is also occasionally termed the Bloodless Revolution, albeit inaccurately. The English Civil War (also known as the Great Rebellion) was still within living memory for most of the major English participants in the events of 1688, and for them, in comparison to that war (or even the Monmouth Rebellion of 1685) the deaths in the conflict of 1688 were few. [...] After being revisited by historians in 1988 —the third centennial of the event— several researchers have argued that the "revolution" was actually a successful Dutch invasion of Britain. The events were unusual because the establishment of a constitutional monarchy (a de facto republic, see Coronation Oath Act 1688) and Bill of Rights meant that the apparently invading monarchs, legitimate heirs to the throne, were prepared to govern with the English Parliament. It is difficult to classify the entire proceedings of 1687–89 but it can be seen that the events occurred in three phases: conspiracy, invasion by Dutch forces and "Glorious Revolution". It has been argued that the invasion aspect had been downplayed as a result of a combination of British pride and successful Dutch propaganda, trying to depict the course of events as a largely internal English affair. As the invitation was initiated by figures who had little influence themselves, the legacy of the Glorious Revolution has been described as a successful propaganda act by William to cover up and justify his successful invasion. The claim that William was fighting for the Protestant cause in England was used to great effect to disguise the military, cultural and political impact that the Dutch regime had on England at the time. The overthrow of James was hailed at the time and ever since as the "Glorious Revolution". Edmund Burke set the tone for over two centuries of historiographical analysis when he proclaimed that "the Revolution was made to preserve our ancient indisputable laws and liberties, and that ancient constitution of government which is our only security for law and liberty." Many historians have endorsed Burke's view, including Macaulay (1848) and more recently John Morrill, who captured the consensus of contemporary historiography well when he declared that "the Sensible Revolution of 1688–89 was a conservative Revolution". On the other hand, Steven Pincus (2009) argues that it was momentous especially when looking at the alternative that James was trying to enact – a powerful centralized autocratic state, using French-style "state-building". England's role in Europe and the country's political economy in the 17th century refutes the view of many late-20th-century historians that nothing revolutionary occurred during the Glorious Revolution of 1688–89. Pincus says it was not a placid turn of events. In diplomacy and economics William III transformed the English state's ideology and policies. This occurred not because William III was an outsider who inflicted foreign notions on England but because foreign affairs and political economy were at the core of the English revolutionaries' agenda. The revolution of 1688-89 cannot be fathomed in isolation. It would have been inconceivable without the changes resulting from the events of the 1640s and 1650s. Indeed, the ideas accompanying the Glorious Revolution were rooted in the mid-century upheavals. Thus, the 17th century was a century of revolution in England, deserving of the same scholarly attention that 'modern' revolutions attract. James II tried building a powerful militarised state on the mercantilist assumption that the world's wealth was necessarily finite and empires were created by taking land from other states. The East India Company was thus an ideal tool to create a vast new English imperial dominion by warring with the Dutch and the Mogul Empire in India. After 1689 came an alternative understanding of economics, which saw Britain as a commercial rather than an agrarian society. The proponents of this view, most famously Adam Smith in 1776, argued that wealth was created by human endeavor and was thus potentially infinite.

The Glorious Revolution of 1688 is considered by some as being one of the most important events in the long evolution of the respective powers of Parliament and the Crown in England. With the passage of the Bill of Rights, it stamped out once and for all any possibility of a Catholic monarchy, and ended moves towards absolute monarchy in the British kingdoms by circumscribing the monarch's powers. These powers were greatly restricted; he or she could no longer suspend laws, levy taxes, make royal appointments, or maintain a standing army during peacetime without Parliament's permission – to this day the Army is known as the "British Army" not the "Royal Army" as it is, in some sense, Parliament's Army and not that of the King. This is, however, a complex issue, as the Crown remains the source of all executive authority in the British army, with legal implications for unlawful orders etc. Since 1689, government under a system of constitutional monarchy in England, and later the United Kingdom, has been uninterrupted. Since then, Parliament's power has steadily increased while the Crown's has steadily declined. Unlike in the English civil war of the mid-seventeenth century, the "Glorious Revolution" did not involve the masses of ordinary people in England (the majority of the bloodshed occurred in Ireland). This fact has led many historians, including Stephen Webb, to suggest that, in England at least, the events more closely resemble a coup d'état than a social revolution. This view of events does not contradict what was originally meant by "revolution": the coming round of an old system of values in a circular motion, back to its original position, as Britain's constitution was reasserted, rather than formed anew. Prior to his arrival in England, the new king William III of England was not Anglican, but rather was a member of the Dutch Reformed Church. Consequently, as a Calvinist and Presbyterian he was now in the unenviable position of being the head of the Church of England, while technically being a Nonconformist. This was, however, not his main motive for promoting religious toleration. More important in that respect was the need to keep happy his Catholic allies in the coming struggle with Louis XIV. Though he had promised legal toleration for Catholics in his Declaration of October 1688, he was ultimately unsuccessful in this respect, due to opposition by the Tories in the new Parliament. The Revolution led to the Act of Toleration of 1689, which granted toleration to Nonconformist Protestants, but not to

Catholics. Catholic emancipation would be delayed for 140 years. The Williamite War in Ireland can be seen as the source of later conflict, including The Troubles of recent times. The Williamite victory in Ireland is still commemorated by the Orange Order for preserving British and Protestant dominance in the country. In North America, the Glorious Revolution precipitated the 1689 Boston revolt in which a well-organised "mob" of provincial militia and citizens successfully deposed the hated governor Edmund Andros, which has been seen as a precedent for the American War of Independence a century later. In New York, Leisler's Rebellion caused the colonial administrator, Francis Nicholson, to flee to England. A third event, Maryland's Protestant Rebellion was directed against the proprietary government, seen as Catholic-dominated. Lord Macaulay's account of the Revolution in The History of England from the Accession of James the Second exemplifies its semi-mystical significance to later generations.

William of Orange might have been an EZ-puppet, and nobody knows to what extent the present Dutch Royalty follows along this path.

CHAPTER 3

Blackmail and Punishment

3.1 Céline Dion

Céline photographed in 1994 and 2000, respectively.

Céline was no doubt unpalatable to EZ: beautiful, feminine, long hair, sometimes wearing 19th century dresses at her performances (like in Italy, for example), pro-life, three children, married once. These are too many virtues in too visible a Christian woman, for EZ to allow her being an example for other Christians. Wikipedia's quotes some of her philanthropic activities:

Dion has actively supported many charity organizations, worldwide. She has promoted the Canadian Cystic Fibrosis Foundation (CCFF) since 1982, and became the foundation's National Celebrity Patron in 1993. She has an emotional attachment to the foundation; her niece Karine succumbed to the disease at the age of sixteen, in Dion's arms. In 2003, she joined a number of other celebrities, athletes, and politicians, including Josh Groban and Yolanda Adams to support "World Children's Day", a global fundraising effort sponsored by McDonald's. The effort raised money from more than 100 nations and benefited orphanages and children's health organizations. In addition, Dion has been a major supporter of the T. J. Martell Foundation, the Diana Princess of Wales Memorial Fund, and many health and educational campaigns. During the aftermath of Hurricane Katrina, Dion donated $1 million to the victims of the storm, and held a fund-raising event for the victims of the 2004 Asian tsunami, which subsequently raised more than $1 million. After the 2008 Sichuan earthquake, Dion donated $100,000 to China Children & Teenagers' Fund and sent a letter showing her consolation and support.

Above the reader can appreciate the result of EZ's revenge: the woman of exquisite heterosexual femininity has changed into a phantasm, and is forced into window-dressing a genderless baby line. All the respective photographs have been deleted in the meantime, by the way. The genderless baby line was just one humiliation more. Now she is forced to have pictures taken with some nipple-covering outfits, which I will spare the reader.

This is not even a shadow of Céline Dion. This is a destroyed woman who went through an unspeakable traumatic experience, which neither the reader nor the writer can possibly fathom. She stands as a symbol for all American actors. Only very few are able to resist EZ: Among them the most famous are Mel Gibson (hardly) and Jim Caviezel (at the price of being eliminated from EZ's Hollywood list for their "Passion of the Christ"), and for similar reasons, Katherine Heigl (who received a series of killing reviews). But what do you expect of the Hollywood career of this other Christian woman, who cherished her virginity until her marriage?

This beautiful woman is 40 years old, and has never been divorced as far as I know (to date she is 51). She does not need a décolleté down to her navel to shine like a pearl, nor does she need to operate her lips, breasts, or hips. She is of Aryan race. EZ should be able to handle this racial detail, for Ivanka is, too. However, she was ousted out of Hollywood because EZ apparently was not able to handle her exemplary role

in movies. She did not mind at all impersonating a self-sacrificing housewife, like in "Love Comes Softly". Was she a bitch during the filming? Ask it to those who can know: Dale Midkiff and Michael Landon jr.

The same holds for all serious Christian actors, and even many honest non-Christian ones, who do not bow for EZ's blackmails. Take Matt Damon, married once, never divorced. If he had some sexual adventures, his wife apparently forgave him. So what do all those dirty dicks and rather selective #MeToo movements comment on? Did #MeToo incriminate Bill Clinton? George Bush sr.? If not so, they had better #YouNeither themselves.

Those who do advance in EZ's "exclusive" demonic clubs, have the choice between torture and "ascension" (read: increasing submission to the devil). Poor Angelina Jolie, she went the whole way up in some super-élite demonic club. This must have been a hell of humiliation for her.[35]

---

[35] EZ despises women, because their sexual appeal reminds them of their lack of virtuosity. EZ only indulges their own women for procreation, and the Gentile ones for whores.

3.2 Pope Benedict XVI

If Pope Benedict XVI had abdicated for reasons of health, he would have asked for a Bavarian Monastery to pray in peace. However, he came up with a rather theoretical, somewhat forced, distinction between the Pope's governing task and his dignity. Of course this distinction exists. However, not everything that is composed remains the same when decomposed.[36] Not even Prof. Dr. Ratzinger can decompose the Pope's governing tasks and his dignity, without destroying papacy. Benedict claimed to have abdicated only from *his governing task* as pastor of his flock, though not from his *papal dignity*, claiming that he would back up his successor with prayer. Such an idea is theological nonsense.

There are but two choices in the Catholic Church: there is either one Pope or no Pope. And with the election of Bergoglio as Ratzinger's successor, there is only one person with Papal dignity. Is the Pope not the visible Head of Christ's Mystical Body, the *Unam, Sanctam, Catholicam et Apostolicam Ecclesiam*? The question arises: how come one of the world's finest theologians utters such nonsense? Did history not make it sufficiently plain that every period with more than one Pope was a period of profound crisis in the Catholic Church?

---

36   This follows from Aristotle's principle of hylemorphism. The Papal right to government follows from his dignity. These two principles relate like potency to act.

Ay, methinks. As we saw Ratzinger slowly getting settled into his new role of Emeritus Pope, clinging as long as possible to his papal dignity, one could already deduce something was very, very wrong. Ratzinger never was the man to claim honor for himself. I consider Emeritus Pope Benedict a true saint: wise, learned, and humble at the time. The only conclusion I can draw from his pieces of theatre, is that he tried to communicate something to Catholicism, as he was being severely blackmailed. Some Catholic journalists shout out: "he is a liar, because he denies being blackmailed!" They'd better look up the definition of blackmail in the dictionary, before writing down such idiocies.

3.3 Pope Francis

Vatican-watcher Simone Varisco wrote in September 2016 that, shortly after the Papal Conclave, Bergoglio had Benedictus' papal ring scratched, symbolizing the end of Benedictus co-regency proposal.[37] In September 2015 Vatican-watcher Maurizio Blondet[38] received a tip from one of his readers to read her website.[39] Blondet believed the information of that website, and wrote that part of Benedict's blackmail consisted in eliminating the Vatican

---

37   http://www.caffestoria.it/tre-anelli-benedetto-xvi-ultime-conversazioni/
38   https://www.maurizioblondet.it/ratzinger-non-pote-ne-vendere-ne-comprare
39   http://sauraplesio.blogspot.it/2015/09/giallo-vaticano.html

from the SWIFT list (a list of non-terrorist countries), which is tantamount to the Vatican's impossibility to buy nor pay. This would put an immediate end to all the Church's philanthropic initiatives. Blondet cannot help but sighing *that the Italian judiciary has that reputation for always following orders from outside Italy.*[40] Blondet's interpretation confirms the 2013 claim of four American Catholics (David Sonnier, Michael Matt, Christopher Ferrara and Chris Jacksonhave) that the money stream from the American Democrat Party to the Vatican had been interrupted weeks before Benedict's abdication, *and had been re-established at the very moment of his officially pronounced abdication.*[41] In their letter to President Trump, these four Americans formally ask Trump to start an investigation concerning Democrat (Soros-Obama-Clinton)[42] meddling with the papal election in 2013. I fear Trump simply ignored their letter. But wait, was the American Democrat Party not always the political "longa manus" of Extreme Zionism?[43]

Maurizio Blondet begins his 2015 masterpiece article with a rectification. In a previous article, he had claimed

---

40   In his own words: "Era la rovina economica, ben preparata da una violenta campagna contro lo IOR, confermata dall'apertura di inchieste penali della magistratura italiana (che non manca mai di obbedire a certi ordini internazionali)"

41   Since the conjurors had already decided who would follow up Pope Benedict, lifting the SWIFT penalty did not need to wait until the newly elected Pope was known

42   William Jasper, Michael Matt

43   called EZ throughout this Decalogue

that the secret Sankt Gallen meetings in Switzerland[44] nullified the election of Jorge Bergoglio as Pope Francis.

He quotes a canonist's reply to his article that the Sankt-Gallen meetings in no way nullifies the legal validity of Bergoglio's election; certainly not, when the meetings have taken place *before* closure. The unknown canonist refers to many cases of secret elector gatherings in the late Middle Ages and the Renaissance.

This is curious indeed. Since the Renaissance (14th to 16th century) there have apparently hardly been secret elector meetings. What happens now, then, that such a meeting suddenly manifests itself, and grossly indecent? I can only conclude that Catholic brainwashing has reached such an extraordinary extent, that Catholics do not even recognize manipulation as it happens under their own eyes! The result is a manifest Catholic invitation to EZ to take over the Catholic pontificate.

Blondet completes his analysis of Benedict's abdication by quoting Luciano Canfora, who demonstrates that Benedict's claim to abdicate because of his age (in the letter "Ingravescente Aetate") contains a large amount of elementary blunders against Latin grammar. Hence, *Benedict cannot possibly be the free author of his Abdication Letter*. Blondet explains these facts, and Emeritus-Pope Benedict's leaving the Vatican

---

44   organized by Italian Cardinal Carlo Maria Martini (who asked euthanasia for himself), and made public by Belgian conjurer Godfried Cardinal Danneels

by helicopter, as a clear sign of the enormous haste EZ had to remove their hated obstacle Ratzinger.

After his election, Bergoglio repeatedly made a fool of himself. First, after the election but still under closure, instead of sinking down in grief (like most elected do, fearing the tremendous responsibility they had preferred not to bear), Bergoglio immediately embraces Cardinal Angelo Scola of Milan, who decided to withdraw his eligibility half-way the election.[45] The second one is even worse. In Fatima he claimed to be the murder victim, the white-clothed martyr alluded to in the writings of sister Lucia. Bergoglio clearly wishes to wipe out the memory of St. John Paul II the Great. Third, he claims the heretical stupidity to "enter history as the one who split up the Catholic Church".[46]

Blondet finalizes his article by denouncing Bergoglio's manifest intentions. On nearly all accounts, Bergoglio follows the Freemasonic agenda:

- his asking Europe to keep importing non-European immigrants, as a sign of love towards the poor – exactly in line with the already published (Sept. 7, 2015), and below reproduced, free-masonic document (signed by 28 Freemasonic Lodges)
- his seeking for a canonic possibility to dismantle a valid matrimony

---

45   Andrea Tornielli
46   Nick Donnelly and Walter Mayr

- his purge of *all* traditional thinkers, like Cardinal Raymond Leo Burke, his three cosignatories of the "dubia"
- his excellent relations with the UN, the US congress, Obama
- his voluntary mediation in Cuba
- his protection of protectors of sexual child abuse (like Cardinal Godfried Danneels protected bishop Roger Vangheluwe)[47]

To this little list one can add a multitude of anti-Catholic moves by Bergoglio. His first papal decisions were to *immediately block all ongoing initiatives of Pope Benedict.*

---

[47]   Roger Joseph Vangheluwe (born 7 November 1936) is the former Bishop of Bruges (Belgium). He gained notoriety after admitting to having sexually abused two nephews over the course of a 15-year period while serving first as a priest and then as bishop, though the admission came after the statute of limitations for the crimes had expired, leaving him beyond the reach of state prosecution.

- he stopped the audit of the IOR bank by PwC,[48] under the guidance of Cardinal Pell;
- he expelled the latter to Australia with a false accusation of child abuse;
- he cancelled the Tribunal against Cardinals and Bishops protecting child abusers;[49]
- he cancelled a deep reform of the Curia;
- he sent home all members of the Papal Congregation for the Family;
- he replaced them by exclusively anti-Catholic agitators in favor of LGBT;
- he had some nice handshakes with rotten celebrities like Arnold Schwarzenegger, implying Bergoglio's support for the mass-killing Kyoto agreements;[50]
- he has a pedophile Italian bishop in mind as his future vicar;
- he invited Paul Ehrlich, an insane abortion activist, for a congress in the Vatican;[51]
- he argues for a European Central Bank;[52]
- he required Matthew Festing to implicate Cardinal Burke in his resignation letter[53]

---

48   Andrea Tornielli
49   Reported by Mark Silk
50   Bjørn Lomborg heavily criticized the Kyoto agreements, not for their lofty goal, but for their dramatic inefficiency
51   Claire Chrétien
52   Antonius Aquinas
53   Jan Bentz, Raymond de Souza: Bergoglio required the demission of Grand Master Festing (Sovereign Military Order of Malta) because he had criticized the spread of condoms by his Order

- IOR served as a money laundering facility for criminals;[54]

According to Bergoglio "A person who thinks only about building walls, wherever they may be, and not building bridges, is not Christian." In Israel Bergoglio did not mention the walls. During the Presidential campaign, Bergoglio glamorously failed to criticize the infamous mass-murderer Hillary Clinton, the alternative for Trump. Moreover, where in the US constitution is it written that the President should be a bridge-builder? Is that not rather what a Pope should do? Does Bergoglio really think he built a bridge towards the Chinese Catholics?

---

54   Alberto di Pisa

To the above slightly more expanded list one should add
that Bergoglio

- opposes the Church teaching on contraception;[55]
- knowingly damaged the Chinese Catholic Church;[56]
- visits Israel in awe, while keeping silent about the
  Israeli toppling of all neighboring countries, thereby
  using genocides like that of ISIS;[57]
- obliges Cardinal Müller to fire his best three men off
  the Congregation for the Doctrine of the Faith;[58]

---

55   Matthew McCusker
56   Cardinal Joseph Zen, ex-bishop of Hong Kong
57   Ed Morrissey
58   Marco Tosatti

COMMUNIQUE DE PRESSE

7 septembre 2015

Déclaration des Obédiences européennes

Les Obédiences maçonniques européennes alarmées par la tragédie vécue par les migrants qui fuient des pays en guerre et en proie à la misère en appellent aux gouvernements européens pour qu'ils mettent en œuvre les politiques communes indispensables à un accueil digne et humain de populations en détresse et en péril. L'incapacité des Etats à surmonter les égoïsmes nationaux est un nouveau signal d'une Europe malade où le chacun pour soi l'emporte sur l'intérêt général.

Les Obédiences maçonniques européennes rappellent que le respect des droits de l'homme et du principe de dignité humaine font partie des principes fondateurs de la construction européenne. C'est sur la base de tels principes que la solidarité entre les nations s'est mise en place. L'esprit de solidarité est encore plus nécessaire au vu des bouleversements qui affectent de nombreuses régions du monde.

Sans revenir sur l'histoire d'un continent qui s'est forgé au gré de nombreuses migrations, les drames présents doivent provoquer une prise de conscience et insuffler des politiques d'accueil innovantes. A défaut, le continent européen sera à terme le théâtre de divisions et de conflits qui précipiteront les peuples dans un nouveau malheur. Il n'en résultera qu'une nouvelle exacerbation des nationalismes.

La tragédie présente doit donc être le creuset d'une renaissance et d'un renouveau du rêve européen. Les Obédiences maçonniques signataires attendent désormais des actes dans lesquels les valeurs de solidarité et de fraternité fondatrices de l'Europe trouvent leur juste expression.

Obédiences signataires

Grand Orient de France
Grande Loge Féminine de France
Grande Loge de France
Fédération Française du Droit Humain
Grande Loge Mixte de France
Grande Loge Mixte Universelle
Ordre Initiatique Traditionnel de l'Art Royal
G.L.R.I S.R.U
Grande Loge Libérale d'Autriche (Autriche)
Grand Orient de Belgique (Belgique

...1...

The Grand List of Grand Losers

Since I am but a physicist, and no historian, I beg your pardon for the many omissions in the above list of grievances. Yet, the 22 points suffice, in my view, to prove that EZ had full control over Benedict's replacement by Bergoglio. While the latter remains the "sweet Christ on earth",[59] whom al Catholics pray for intensely, *it is crucial for Catholics to know the difference between filially criticizing what the Pope does, especially when his actions or words have all external appearances of mortal sin, on one hand, and stupidly disputing his legitimacy as the Pope of all Catholicism, on the other.*

As far as Bergoglio's possible future Vicar (Vincenzo Paglia) is concerned: he took the initiative to fully cover his church roof with homosexual and pedophile figures, headed by a resurrected Christ in Adam's clothing. Bergoglio was soooooooh immensely satisfied with that masterpiece, that he first appointed him bishop of Terni, and president of the Pontifical Council of the Family. Shortly afterwards, on the 17th of August in 2017, Bergoglio further elevated him to president of the Pontifical Academy for Life and Grand Chancellor of the "Pontifical Institute John Paul II for the Studies Concerning Matrimony and Family."

Compare that to the fate of all orthodox Cardinals: ejected *stante pede*, often with a knife in their backs.[60]

---

59   St. Catherine of Siena
60   The four *Dubia* writers (among whom Cardinal Burke), Pope
       Benedict XVI, Cardinal Sarah (whom Bergoglio forbade to
       publish his own web pages), and so many others orthodox
       pillars of the Catholic Church: they all suffered at least a
       public smear campaign, the worst being that of Cardinal Pell.
       In the case of Pope Benedict XVI, Bergoglio even has the
       hypocrisy to ask him to comment on some Letter of his, next
       has Benedict's original comment tampered with, and finally
       publishes a tiny, tampered part of Benedict's theological
       study. With what goal? To suggest that Pope Benedict
       approves of Bergoglio's renovation.

Yes, my dear Catholics, we do have to pray much more for this Pope, because no single past Pope has been so profoundly grasped by a devil. A little insignificant one, though. Bergoglio lacks the intellect to require a significant one.

CHAPTER 4

Feminism in the Garbage Can

This chapter tries to explain why "modern" (post-pill) feminism is so harshly humiliated during the last decade.

4.1 Lilleslåtten in Awe for Nesheim

Let me reproduce parts of a 2018 article for the Norwegian gender Newsmagazine *Kilden*, written by journalist Mari Lilleslåtten:[61]

> Twenty per cent of Norwegian women between the age of sixteen and forty-four are on the pill. The contraceptive pill has been in use in Norway for fifty years, but there are still insecurity and myths related to its use and side effects. Today, twenty per cent of all fertile women in Norway

---

61   http://kjonnsforskning.no/en/2018/02/contraceptive-pill-story-sexual-liberation-and-dubious-research-methods

are on the pill. The fact that all women have the
right to information about and access to the right
type of contraception is self-evident. But this has
not always been the case.

These candid lines illustrate Lilleslåtten's ingenuousness,
or brainwashing, or ideological blindness, however one
wishes to call it. The passage is internally inconsistent.
How can there still be insecurity and myths related to the
pill's use, after fifty years of use, with a population
percentage of 20%? I mean, this is not even an academic
problem, but mere tavern-billing: Simply order the
measured numbers.

Every possible difficulty one might encounter is
directly imputable to the pharmaceutical industries. So
what are you waiting for, Norway?[62] Do you accept that
the pharmaceutical industries get away with their hiding
the numbers? Or do you finally wake up from your
lethargy, and claim the civil right to know what kind of
poison your daughters are taking in order to sexually
satisfy their boyfriends without unwanted consequences?
Mari goes on:

"I graduated from medical school the same year
as the contraceptive pill appeared in 1967. I

---

62   This kind of collective ingenuousness is not exclusively
      Norwegian, of course: the same happens all over the globe.

remember it so well; it was like a revolution!" These are the words of Britt Ingjerd Nesheim, professor emerita and retired senior consultant at the Women's Clinic at Ullevål University Hospital and University of Oslo. "Having access to a contraceptive that was secure made it possible to decide not to have children if you didn't want it. The opportunity to securely control your own sexuality and childbirths was something completely new." According to her, the new contraceptive was first met with skepticism. "The medicines authorities, and health director Karl Evang in particular, were skeptical with regards to putting a pill out on the market that had been subject to so little research. And he was right too; frightfully little research had been carried out." [...] When the pill was introduced, we knew little about side effects and the effects it might have on women's long-term health. "It would never have been approved under today's system!" It took seven years from the pill was first introduced as contraception for women in the US until Norwegian women could ask their doctor about the new pills. Norway was careful, and waited longer than both Germany and the other Scandinavian countries. However, in 1963, the pill reached the nation, but not as contraception. "I

haven't been able to find out what the physicians'
desktop reference said about the pill at the time,
but it was registered as a means for regulating
women's menstruation. Yet under the table, many
were probably prescribed the pill as a
contraceptive," says Nesheim.

In spite of waiting longer than other Scandinavian
countries (congratulations, Karl Evang), nobody yet knew
about side effects? This can only mean that the ban on
information was global. That, on turn, has the simplest
explanation[63] by assuming that there was but a single
bank that both financed the pill development, and
controlled the information rights of the pill side effect
statistics. Obviously, no other bank than Rothschild's EZ
had such powers and ambitions.

Otherwise, one should come up with at least a shred
of evidence that *ALL pharmaceutical companies selling
the pill concerted their policies, and somehow,
miraculously, managed to influence the legislative
powers **in all western countries**, in order to render
information concerning the pill's side effects inaccessible
to civilians. Once done, calculate the odds of such a
fantastic super-conspiracy, and of the pharmaceutical
industries freely interfering with legislation.* Just

---

63   Of course, the stupid (read: governmental) conspiracy
      theorists will tell you that *all pharmaceutical industries* made
      a secret deal

remember the tobacco industry, and tell me the difference.

Silence? Well, the difference is that the smoker willingly and knowingly poisons herself, while the abortive girl willingly though *unknowingly* poisons not only herself *but also* her baby.[64] Where is the justice in this sordid business? You yell at smokers who hardly harm anybody (just let them pay any lung operations from their own pocket), and keep your mouths shut about liquor self-poisoning, drug self-poisoning, and pill-self-and-progeny-poisoning?

I feel as if I were asking questions to mentally retarded, with a single brain cell allowing them to write idiotic texts on cigarette packages. Candid Lilleslåtten next asks Nesheim:

Would the contraceptive pill have been invented without pressure from the feminist movement?

Dear Mari Lilleslåtten: there *existed no 2018-kind of feminism before the invention of the contraceptive pill.* In other words, the pill converted healthy feminism into a pathologic disease. That was what the pill was meant for

---

64   This baby is no less a human than all adults, of course. With the same human rights. And an extra one: to be born in a family with happily wed father and mother. If a pregnant girl failed to provide these, she should not kill the baby. Am I supposed to kill a beggar after I failed to show him my due respect?

in the first place! One only has to calculate with what an amazing publicity budget the pill was introduced, to realize who could possibly spit that out. And do not be so dumb as pointing at the pharmaceutical giants. They could not have made such an inversion in a product that the whole western society previously thought of as pure evil.

Gregory Pincus and John Rock developed the first contraceptive pill, but the methods in use at the time, in the 1950s, would not have passed today's guidelines for research ethics. "It's a paradox," says Nesheim. "The pill is fantastic, but it has been created under dubious circumstances." The article, and the research, was undocumented – in other words, he cheated. Pincus and Rock experimented on animals, but also on women. They handed out the first test pills to poor women in Puerto Rico who wanted to avoid pregnancies. But they also tested the pills on women in Boston who came to see their doctor about infertility problems. These women wanted children, but were infertile. Rock wrote in an article about the experiment that other research had shown how large portions of progestins might be used as a cure against infertility. But when Nesheim looked at the references in the article more closely, she discovered something conspicuous: "He referred to an article 'in preparation'. The article, and the research, was undocumented – in other words, he cheated." Through the experiments with the childless women, Rock and Pincus were able to prove that progestins hinder the ovulation, which enabled them to study what effects this had on the womb lining. Among other things, they found that the bleedings became irregular when the women were given a lot of progestin, which they then tried to regulate by adding oestrogen. "In this way, they tried out different combinations of the two hormones before they eventually ended up with the product that was launched as the world's first contraceptive pill: Enovid." The unsuspected guinea pigs who had sought help from the doctor in order to get pregnant did not receive any assistance to that end.

Oh, what a romantic story this is, of heroic knight efforts to rescue the threatened, defenseless princess.

The pill was approved and introduced to the American market on a very weak scientific basis with regards to possible side effects. In the beginning, a new experiment was carried out in Puerto Rico. But the results of the experiment were worthless, according to Nesheim. "What can you expect, really? The intentions were perhaps good, but at the same time, the researchers did not consider the women and their situation. The women failed to take the pills at the right time of the day, and many dropped out of the study. They had chosen Puerto Rico because the legislation there was weak. They could thus carry out experiments there that were difficult to get permission for everywhere else."

Puerto Rico? Weren't your own wives happy to serve your purposes, Rock and Pincus? And what about all the other women in your county? There is something rotten in Denmark...

A lot of research has been done on the contraceptive pill since then. Control-based studies, register-based studies and qualitative research may provide knowledge on how the pill affects the health of those who use it. "In a way, all women have been guinea pigs for the development of the contraceptive pill," says Nesheim. After the pill had been on the market for a while, a few women who used it suffered from blood clots, and some suspected that they might have been caused by the new contraceptive.

It was discovered that the hormones increased the risk of blood clots, and the combination was changed. The first pill contained 150 micrograms of oestrogen; today it only contains between 20 and 40 micrograms.

Only professional assassins are able to speak about their victims as non-personal things. Toward the end of the article, suddenly a significant number pops up, which somehow managed to escape EZ's all-seeing eye.

The number of suicides and suicide attempts are two to three times higher among women who use the pill. The risk she [Nesheim] describes is estimated through research on women on the contraceptive pill compared to control groups of women who are not on the pill. Register-based surveys also contribute to the study of health risks connected to the use of the pill. Possible psychological side effects of the pill are harder to measure than the physical. "Many complain about mood swings. The fact that many feel depressed is difficult to measure. But a Danish register-based study appeared recently. This study shows that the number of suicides and suicide attempts are two to three times higher among women who use the pill. This particularly applies to young women. It thus appears that the depression that many women complain about is very real, and may have dire consequences." "You need to be aware of this possible side effect and stop taking the pill if it gets serious," she emphasizes.

Nesheim has the guts to talk in a thoroughly disparaging way about young girls who use her poison! Oh sure, she has nothing to hide. She openly admits that her victims might experience heavy depressions,[65] and even proposes, for free, her philanthropic advice that those victims should stop taking the pill when aware of depression! Nesheim is no doubt an authoritative academician with an impressive CV. Yet she obviously hides her professional knowledge that in depressed people *awareness is not at all comparable to awareness in healthy people. She* might recognize depression instantaneously, from behind her desk, *cleansed of any kind of poison.*[66] However, a depressed person is sick of hearing that she is depressed, and only wishes to die in peace. I suggest that Nesheim be brought to justice for crimes against humanity.

Lilleslåtten's 2018 Kilden article concludes with a final deep sigh, namely, the wish that also men participate

65   Her poison pill leads to a threefold suicide rate with respect to girls not taking the pill

66   With Nesheim's knowledge, it is hard to believe she ever took the poison herself.

in the chemical, mental, and moral pains of having sex without the risk of conception:

> Then the question remains whether this revolutionary pill will also be available for men? "A contraceptive pill for men has been under testing. It contains progestin, which hinders the production of sperm cells. But it also reduces the production of testosterone, which then needs to be added. Whereas women's pill contains progestin and oestrogen, the contraceptive pill for men will contain progestin and testosterone." After fifty years with the pill that gives Norwegian women full freedom to control their own reproduction, the contraceptive pill for men is overdue. But in theory, the revolution may come, also for men.

4.2 The Ideal of Feminism

Although I fully agree with the general equal-risk equal-pain principle when two individuals join in a single adventure, I would beg Mari Lilleslåtten to consider the mere facts

- that men want sex more often than women do (this is hard-wired into human genes in the course of billions of years of sexual evolution, whence forget about changing this behavior);
- that men dominate women over the same archeological period, and will always be doing so, though *only due to their physical strength and evolutionarily S-wired brains*, not due to intellectual superiority.

The highest form of social equality women can reach, and I sincerely hope they succeed in that endeavor, is by means of intellectual dominance. That is accessible in practice, though only on a few specific conditions, two of those being lifting the ban on sex-separated high-school education, and housewife remuneration.[67]

I had but a short look at video fragments of discussions between silly defenders of modern (post-pill) feminism, with well-known debaters like Milo Yiannopoulos, Jordan Peterson, Ben Shapiro, and Gavin McInnis. In this section, I wish to discuss but a single aspect of these videos: Milo and many other professional provocateurs have visible troubles not to laugh aloud at the continuous pitiful utterances of an EZ-faked young feminist. The EZ-fakes are clearly recognizable, by the fact that the feminist is a young, attractive girl, that behaves more like hitting on the provocateur than debating with

---

67   This is the topic of my book on feminism

him. The non-fakes are recognizable by the fact that the feminist is frustrated, angry, old, and "less attractive", to put it mercifully.

In both cases it is obvious that EZ decided to let modern feminism down. That leaves me with two questions: first, how would that fit into their strategy, and second, are Americans aware that their moral judgement flaps like a leaf in the wind? For your information, the declaration of human rights does not. This affects

- pre-pill feminism
- so-called "racist police violence": vitriolic ideologies like "Black Lives Matter" and "the Occupy Movement" are as hate-instilling as the Ku Klux Klan (Sheriff David Clarke),
- rudeness and murder among black youngsters (Candice Owens),
- violent hard-core leftism on nearly all UC campuses, initiated by both students and thoroughly extremist staff and board (Ben Shapiro).

Hence, let me delve a bit deeper, and reformulate my question. Who is able to swap around the American general opinion within a few years? Feminists were heroes ten years ago, and now they serve as pissing poles on American television channels?

I think of feminism as a movement with eminently positive possibilities. Too bad, it never came up with a single practical idea of how to get women equally respected in society as men. All their proposals are fueled by frustration instead of by true love for financially poorly doing women. The republican and democrat proposals are both largely wanting, too.

According to some republican Christians, the basis of society's appreciation of women is their being *extremely miraculous* baby-factories. They are extremely miraculous beings indeed, but baby factories *they are certainly not, nor ever will be.* These are nothing but wet dreams of Christian fools.

On the other hand, according to the majority of liberals, the basis of society's appreciation of women is their being *like men.* Which they are obviously not, either. This is even dumber than the position of Christian fools.

In Section 4.1 we already mentioned that pill-free women have a suicide rate one third that of pill-taking women. The latter forming 20% of Norwegian fertile women, and women having a 5 times smaller suicide rate than men, without the pill the suicide rate would be 1:6 for women to men. From these numbers it is immediately obvious which is the psychologically stable sex, and which the psychologically weak sex. Hence, it should be obvious to the reader which sex EZ needs to destabilize first.

With these thoughts in mind, I nevertheless believe that traditional feminism did enormous harm to society, not because of their endeavor, but because of the solution they came up with to reach that endeavor. EZ brainwashed them into believing they had only two alternatives: the democratic and the republican solutions. Since both solutions are extremely woman-destabilizing, traditional feminism turned many normal girls and adult women into frustrates, whence many families into nut houses. Now that EZ definitively managed to get female degradation solidly rooted in American society, feminism is not EZ's priority anymore. Hence, there goes feminism... straight into the garbage can. No panic, my dear TV public! Now LGBT will happily take the place of traditional feminism, not knowing that they will follow the same itinerary: Once the LGBT ideal is firmy established in American society, EZ will throw LGBT in the garbage can, with the obvious consequence that many honorable LGBT's will be pissed off mercilessly on TV (I guess, within 20 years from now).

Who has the guts to place oneself in the devil's shoes, can easily predict the following EZ-moves, one by one. After LGTBQIA+, the concept of marriage will no doubt be extended to include all juridical inter-mammal sexual relationships. Once the revolutionary insight in inter-mammal happiness has been thoroughly established in society, EZ will declare war on intellectuals, just as they successfully experimented with in Cambodia: they perfectly know how to make intellectuals suspect for the great public. Once the intellectuals have been mass-murdered, and society's average IQ has fallen some significant points, the next category of suspects are all lower-IQ individuals who lack addictions (alcohol, games, drugs). Remove them from society, too, and what is left is the ideal society where EZ can freely fish for imbecile, substance-addicted, groggy slaves.

Modern feminism, whose birth certificate was the Nazi-practice of using Puerto Rican women as guinea pigs for testing a venom, was but a first step in EZ's war on the last bastion of Gentile morality, which is the Catholic Church.

APPENDIX 1

Protocols of the Meetings of the Learned Elders of Zion

Due to the high number of pages of the EZ Protocols, we relegated them to a separate book called "Appendices to the Snake". Here you only find the table of contents.

Protocol I	The Basic Doctrine
Protocol II	Economic Wars
Protocol III	Methods of Conquest
Protocol IV	Materialism Replaces Religion
Protocol V	Despotism and Modern Progress
Protocol VI	Take-Over Technique
Protocol VII	World-Wide Wars
Protocol VIII	Provisional Government
Protocol IX	Re-education
Protocol X	Preparing for Power
Protocol XI	The Totalitarian State
Protocol XII	Control of the Press
Protocol XIII	Distractions
Protocol XIV	Assault on Religion
Protocol XV	Ruthless Suppression
Protocol XVI	Brainwashing
Protocol XVII	Abuse of Authority
Protocol XVIII	Arrest of Opponents
Protocol XIX	Rulers and People
Protocol XX	Financial Program
Protocol XXI	Loans and Credit
Protocol XXII	Power of Gold
Protocol XXIII	Instilling Obedience
Protocol XXIV	Qualities of the Ruler

APPENDIX 2

Henry Ford's "International Jew"

Due to the quite extensive work "International Jew" by Henry Ford, founder of Ford Motor Company, we relegated it to the same book "Appendices to the Snake". Here you only find the table of contents.

APPENDIX 3

Exodus

The below list of expulsions of Jews shows how many times this happened in only 2000 years of history.[68]

---

135 B.C   Antiochus Epiphanes desecrates Second Jewish Temple; leading to Hasmonean Revolt against the Greeks.

70 A.D.   Titus took Jerusalem - second revolt. Over one million Jews killed.

136 A.D.   580,000 men destroyed, 985 towns destroyed - third revolt.

300 A.D.   Purim festival celebrating God's deliverance to Mordecai and the Jews

---

through Esther and the fasting. Lies spread that Jews kill Christians for sacrifice. Emperor Severus also said the Jews purchased 90,000 Christians to kill them.

306 A.D.   Council in Spain banned Christians & Jews meeting or marrying.

325 A.D.   Constantine changed the celebration of Easter on the calendar so that it did not coincide with the Jewish Passover.

379 A.D.   [...]

395 A.D.   [...]

415 A.D.   [...] Accusation of Ritual murder by the Jews during Purim. Christians confiscated synagogues in Antioch.

717 A.D.   Jews had to wear special yellow garb. Originated in Islam.

1012 A.D. Emperor Henry II of Germany expels Jews from Mainz, the beginning of persecutions against Jews in Germany.

1096 A.D. First Crusade. Crusaders massacre the Jews of the Rhineland.

1144 A.D. First recorded blood libel. In Norwich it was alleged that the Jews had "bought a

Christian child before Easter, tortured him with all the tortures wherewith our Lord was tortured and on Friday hanged him on a rood in hatred of our Lord." (England) [...]

1190 A.D.   Massacre of Jews in England.

1215 A.D.   The Jewish badge introduced.

1240 A.D.   Talmud burned in France.

1290 A.D.   Jews expelled from England.

1298 A.D.   Massacre of thousands in Germany, in 146 localities.

1306 A.D.   Talmud burned in France.

1290 A.D.   Jews expelled from England.

1298 A.D.   Massacre of thousands in Germany, in 146 localities.

1306 A.D.   Expulsion from France.

1348 A.D.   Jews blamed for the black death. Charge laid to the Jews that they poisoned the wells to kill Christians.

1389 A.D.   Massacres in Bohemia and Spain.

1421 A.D.   270 Jews burned at the stake. In the 14th and 15th centuries the Inquisition was more intense because the Church and State joined forces. Just being Jewish guaranteed persecution

1480 A.D. Inquisition in Spain - Jews and Christians
           burned at the stake.

1483 A.D. Expulsions from Warsaw, Sicily, Lithuania,
           Portugal.

1492 A.D. All Jews expelled from Spain.

1506 A.D. Murders in Lisbon - 4000, "conversos",
           men, women, and children thrown from
           windows to street mobs below, due to
           preaching by Dominicans against the Jews.

1510 A.D. Jews expelled from Brandenburg, Germany

1516 A.D. Venice initiates the ghetto, the first in
           Christian Europe.

1544 A.D. The Reformation. At the end of Martin
           Luther's life the German reformer vilified
           the Jews in violent pamphlets which could
           not fail to exert their influence. But
           because Calvinists were steeped in Old
           Testament theology, the Dutch people
           respected the Jews as "the Chosen"
           people; and were not anti-Semitic in their
           faith. The reformation was a time of
           turmoil as the Roman Church and feudalism
           lost their supremacy. There was a rising up
           of Nationhood and Luther was a German

nationalist. The Talmud was seized and burned everywhere by Papal authority. Jews in Catholic countries and Polish Jews suffered greatly. Luther's anti-Semitic writings were later used in anti-Semitic literature.

1553 A.D. Rome seized and burned the Talmud by order of the Pope.

1559 A.D. 12,000 copies of Talmud burned in Milan.

1569 A.D. Pope Pius V ordered all Jews out of the Papal states.

1593 A.D. Expulsions from Italy and Bavaria.

1598 A.D. Ritual murder charge that sent three Jews to their deaths. Execution of the supposed guilty was done by quartering. (In his book the "Birth of the Prison" Michel Foucault describes at length the quartering of a condemned man in 1757. It was done eventually by six horses instead of the four original ones and other means had to come in to play due to the failure even of six horses as the prisoners' limbs were tied to ropes harnessed to the horses. Each horse pulled in a different direction. One horse fell to the ground unsuccessfully. Knives had to be used for severing...)

1614 A.D. Jews attacked and driven out of Frankfurt, Germany.

1624 A.D. Ghetto established in Ferrara, Italy.

1648 A.D. Leader of the Cossacks, in the Ukraine massacres 100,000 Jews and destroyed 300 communities.

1655 A.D. Massacres of Jews in war against Sweden & Russia by Poland.

1715 A.D. Pope Pius VI issues edict against Jews.

1768 A.D. 20,000 Jews in Poland killed.

1805 A.D. Massacre of Jews in Algeria.

1840 A.D. Blood Libel in Damascus.

1853 A.D. Blood Libel in Russia.

1858 A.D. The Mortara Case: Catholics abduct a 7 yr. old Jewish child. A Catholic servant baptized a Jewish child when the child was seriously ill and the church of Rome seized the child. Outcry had no effect on the Pope.

1879 A.D. Word anti-Semitism comes into existence.

1881 A.D. Pogroms began. The word is of Russian origin. It designates attack, accompanied by destruction, looting of property, murder, rape. There were three major outbreaks in Russia. The word designates more particularly the attacks carried out by the Christian population. Each pogrom surpassed the other in savagery. Kiev, Odessa: Here murder of whole families was a common occurrence. Partial data are available for 530 communities in which 887 major pogroms and 349 minor pogroms occurred. There were 60,000 dead and several times that many were wounded.

1882 A.D. First Anti-Jewish Congress Held in Dresden, Germany.

1894 A.D. Alfred Dreyfus Trial in France. Details follow further on in this summary

1903 A.D. Appearance of a new issue of the "protocols of the elders of Zion". in Russia. This specter of a worldwide Jewish conspiracy aiming at reducing the Gentiles to slavery or extermination loomed up in the medieval Christian imagination and grew out of legends about well poisonings and plague spreading. It was concocted in

Paris by an unknown author working for the Russian secret police. It was an alleged conference of the leaders of World Jewry. It was translated into all the world languages. In 1963 a Spanish edition was published. During World War II, the Protocols of the elders of Zion became an implicit justification for the genocide of the Jews and Nazi propaganda relied on them until the last days of the Third Reich. Smaller pamphlets of it have been distributed in B.C. 1983 published in California... Required reading in most Arab countries, in schools, to this day.

1905 A.D. Russian pogroms continue. Also in Morocco, Ukraine, 300 dead.

1919 A.D. 3000 Jews killed in Hungarian pogroms.

1920 A.D. Appearance of Adolph Hitler. Also Henry Ford the 1st believes the Protocols; and publishes anti-Jewish articles in his newspaper, the Dearborn Independent.

1925 A.D. "Mein Kamph" [sic] appears. Hitler's Plan published in Germany.

1933 A.D. Hitler appointed chancellor in Germany.

1935 A.D.   Hitler writes his Nuremberg Laws which lead to his Final Solution.

1938 A.D.   Burning in Austria & Germany of Synagogues. Jews sent to concentration camps. Beginnings of the Holocaust.

1939 A.D.   Germany overruns Poland.

1940 A.D.   Gassing, shootings in Polish Ghettos (Jewish).

1941 A.D.   Expulsion of Jews from the German Reich to Poland. Riots against Jews in Iraq.

1942 A.D.   Mass transports of Jews to Belgium & Holland.

1944 A.D.   Extermination of Hungarian Jews.

1945 A.D.   Holocaust Final Count: 6,000,000 Jews slaughtered.

1946 A.D.   Pogroms in Poland - 42 Jews murdered.

1948 A.D.   Birth of The State of Israel. Also Jewish intellectuals shot in Russia.

1952 A.D.   Jews murdered by Communists, and others disappear. Prague trials. Murder of Yiddish intellectuals in Russia and many sent to work camps.

1956 A.D.   Jews expelled out of Egypt.

1967 A.D.　Six Day War. Also new publication of Elders of Zion in Arabic.

1968 A.D.　Emigration of last remaining Jews in Poland.

1969 A.D.　Jews Executed in Iraq.

1970 A.D.　Beginning of imprisonment in Russia of prisoners of conscience. ("Refuseniks")

1980 A.D.　Russian imprisonments carry on throughout the 70's to the 80's.

1982 A.D.　War in Lebanon begins after many years of terrorist attacks against the Jews in the Upper Galilee area from the vantage point of Beaufort Castle. Many Lebanese killed over long period of time, but was ignored by the News Media. War in Lebanon gets slanted coverage.

1983 A.D.　Word from Christians in Israel that the PLO planned their next battleground to be Canada via Quebec. Documented proof that Russia planned in 1982 to attack Israel.

Until here the list from the Jewish page. I replaced parts of the text by square brackets [...], whenever the claims reached a certain level of anti-historical stupidity. The list, which reads like a long list of grieves against the rest of

humanity, brings one major question to my mind, the
fourth one in the below list of questions.

- First: In absolute numbers, many more Armenians
  were tortured to death by the Young Turks than Jews
  by the Nazi's. The Jews ending up in concentration
  camps were mostly hungered to death, and all
  Armenians thirsted to death. Would the six million
  Jewish victims have preferred to die in the Armenian
  holocaust, had they had the choice?[69]
- Second: the list of grieves does not differ at all from
  the Armenian list of grieves. So how come the
  Armenian, the Hutu and Tutsi, and thousands of
  others genocides disappeared from the history books,
  while the WW II Jewish mass-murder even has its
  own name?
- Third: why is the list so prominently anti-Catholic,
  when all post-war Jews of significance did not know
  how to thank the Catholic Church for its help, both by
  individual faithful and by the Hierarchy?
- Fourth: why were all other genocides unique in
  history, while Jewish genocides and expulsions seem
  a rule rather than an exception?

---

69   There exist people who really believe that the Nazi's would go
      to that length and lordship as to have Jews gassed to death,
      which is about the most painless dead a healthy person can
      wish to die.

The usual answer to the last question (the first three being rhetoric) is that the Jewish *always* willfully self-isolated because of their deeply rooted conviction to be God's chosen people. Only legally circumcised Jews could form part of that chosen people. To the hosting people, this attitude seemed, true or not, both treacherous and arrogant.

To this usual answer I would like to add that the Jewish Sacred book of Exodus is one big historical narration of the genocide of all peoples living in today's Israel, with that of the Amalekites being the best documented one. *Moses repeatedly instructed his army chief, Joshua, to exterminate all adults, children, and animals he found in the Holy Land, while keeping nothing for personal booty.*

Not for mere personal antipathy, prophet Samuel replaced the first Jewish King (Shaul) by David because Shaul had asked ransom money in return for the captured Amalekite King. Hence, the narration is not only historical, but quite consistent, too.

Whatever is true about all the above, even this "extended usual answer" is hardly sufficient to explain the WW II genocide, let alone all other attempted genocides on the Jews in history. So it does not satisfy me at all. Therefore, I propose the following historic model:

- First, there exist two very different kinds of Jews. The large majority of Jews are virtuous and God-fearing. A very small minority descends from the Sadducees:

the very mafia that required Jesus' death at the cross from Pontius Pilate. This mafia, which I call EZ throughout the decalogue, did not mysteriously disappear anno 33 (minus a tiny calendar correction). It had enough wealth and direct communication with the Roman authorities to escape the full destruction of Jerusalem. What few virtuous Jews know, is that the very Sadducees convinced the ordinary Jews not ever to leave the Holy City, but rather die from exhaustion and famine. This attitude, so generously adopted by Mussolini two centuries later,[70] was to be a constant practice from that time onwards. EZ mastered it so well, that they got away with it two millennia long, and are still getting away with it, due to the ingenuousness of the ordinary Jews, which is mind-boggling, and the ingenuousness of all other people around, both Christians and non-Christians.

- This explanation might be hard to believe, but it explains the above Jewish list of grieves in all detail. It is not the ordinary, virtuous Jews who stole children to ritually sacrifice them to the Moloch. No, it was the Sadducee mafia, and they did it in utmost secrecy. The ingenuous Christians never were able to distinguish between EZ and the ordinary Jews. But how were they to know, given that the ordinary Jews

---

70   "Armiamoci e partite!" he said to the Italians. Translated: "Let us take arms, and off you go!" This might also be an Italian joke, rather than an historical fact.

always wanted to live in ghettos, and always refused intimacy with heathens?

- Catholic theology has very simple and clear ideas about the Moloch, or Satan. It is nothing but the most beautiful of all fallen angels. For the tiniest bit of injustice to occur on earth, Satan always must ask God's permission to cause it. And why would an infinitely merciful God not *always* refuse Satan's requests? Well, because God is not only infinitely merciful, but also infinitely just. It would not be just towards a free living being created by God, *to deny all its requests*. Hence, from time to time, God allows the Satan to have it its way, as is made very plain in the Sacred Book of Job. Finally, *God's omnipotence is able to draw more good from Satan's evil*. This must infuriate Satan time and again.

- Another theological simplicity that Catholics seem to have a hard time grasping, is that Satan is not stupid, nor inner divided. Hence, it does not wage war against God, by grasping as many human souls out of God's hands as possible,[71] in an inner divided way, as if evil were fighting evil. In many cases it seems like that, but only to fool the ingenuous. No, Satan has a very strict and hierarchical command chain, as unified as it can possibly be. Now, my dear ingenuous Catholic, please tell me, who would be the human

---

71   the angelic fall has already happened, so nothing left to do
      there for Satan

commander in chief of Satan? Mao? Hitler? They left nothing but destruction, and certainly not a school of thought. So who else might be a candidate?

- Catholic theologians never say it explicitly, but they do know the maxim: "deepest falls the one who refuses God's highest grace".[72] With this maxim in mind, there is no other commander in chief possible but the very Godfather of the Sadducee mafia.

The above model explains why Rothschild's financial imperium is about ten times the financial size of the USA. It explains all the acts of terror in the past two centuries, including 9/11. It explains why the US policy in the Middle East is continuous across all possible US presidents, and equally was in the far East. It explains why all US Americans had to lie about their foreign wars, the worst ones being those who are awarded a Nobel Prize of Stupidity.

Excuses. I meant Peace.

---

72   A similar pattern of repeated expulsions from every possible
      European country is quite clear from the history of the
      Jesuits, too. What would the Jesuits have in common with the
      Jews? Well, everything. The large majority of the Jesuits are
      virtuous people. A small minority exclusively busies itself with
      trying to influence earthly political rulers. This minority
      prefers its own interests to those of the Company of Jesus.
      The majority is too intellectual to communicate well with
      ordinary people. Hence, all ingredients are available for
      repeated expulsions.